THE MARATHON BOOK

THE MARATHON BOOK

Neil Wilson
Andy Etchells
Bruce Tulloh

Virgin Books

First published in Great Britain
in 1982 by Virgin Books Ltd,
95-99 Ladbroke Grove, London W11 1PG

ISBN 0 907080 33 2

Printed in Great Britain by
Richard Clay Ltd, Suffolk
Production services by
Book Production Consultants, Cambridge

Typeset by Padnall Printers, London
Designed by Ray Hyden
Cover illustration by Bernard Fallon

'One can but hope that the tragic examples of
Dorando in the 1908 Olympics and now of Jim Peters
will have at last convinced world officials that
marathon racing is not a sport but an excessive
physical strain which should not be tolerated in
any civilised country.'

A Doctor writing in the Daily Mail, August 10, 1954.

'In years to come Marathon Day will eclipse Boat Race
Day and could even upstage Derby Day.'

Daily Mail, March 30, 1981.

THE AUTHORS

NEIL WILSON makes a perfect foil to his co-authors' vast experience in running marathons. He has never run one and can only claim to have dreams one day of doing so. But at least the inspiration of working with Tulloh and Etchells persuaded him to take the first real steps along the road. For the first time since school, he is running for more than a bus. Neil is the athletics correspondent for the *Daily Mail*, he has covered three Olympic Games, several European and Commonwealth Games and was editor of the British Olympic Association's Official Report of the Montreal Games.

ANDY ETCHELLS is a lifelong club runner who competes for Ilford AC and, occasionally, for his 'second-claim' clubs, Manchester HAC and Thames Hare and Hounds. A double blue at Oxford, he captained the athletics and cross country teams and was President of the University Blues Committee. In 1979 he became founder-editor of *Jogging Magazine*, which changed its name in 1980 to *Running*. He has run marathons in Great Britain, the USA and Finland and has a best time of 2:29:12. Much of his time these days is spent advising beginners on training programmes.

BRUCE TULLOH won the European 5,000m Championship in 1962 and was an international for nine consecutive years at all distances from one mile to 10,000m on the track and up to 20 miles in road and cross country events. During this time he set several British and European records. In 1969, he ran across the USA from Los Angeles to New York in a record time of 65 days. He coached the Kenyan athletics team, including Kip Keino and Mike Boit, prior to the 1972 Olympics. He teaches Biology at Marlborough College and has been coaching successful school teams for 15 years in Kenya, Britain and most recently in the USA. He writes a training column for *Running* magazine and his previous books include: *Tulloh On Running*, *The Long Distance Running Handbook* (with Martin Hyman), *Four Million Footsteps*, *Naturally Fit* and *The Complete Jogger*. Bruce made his marathon debut in 1979 and in 1981, at the age of 46, ran 2:33.

Contents

Introduction

Athletics, the British coach Tom McNab once wrote, is a series of fantasies bounded by rigid rules, and of that series the marathon is the greatest fantasy of all.

Little more than 10 years ago it would have been sufficient almost to run through the streets of the capital cities of the world in shorts and a vest to be thought certifiable. At best those who did run received coarse comments and canine incisors for their pains and, not unnaturally, performed their practises, if not in private, at least discreetly after dark or soon after dawn.

Today, tens of thousands practise it quite openly, public roads in the busiest quarters are closed for them and whole cities turn out to applaud them. Running has become the preoccupation of a generation and the marathon its ultimate challenge.

What was once considered the toughest event on the Olympic programme and the preserve of a few highly-trained, suitably-constructed athletes is now the dream of men, women and children, of every class and creed and of every age. What began as an American dream, another new horizon, a mountain they could build themselves when every mountain had been climbed, is now an international phenomenon.

So what is this marathon that has swept through North America, Europe and now half of the world? In simple terms it is a race over a distance chosen for no good reason between runners who are largely incapable of winning it to commemorate an event which almost certainly never took place.

Historically it is not as old as the telephone, about the same age as the motor car and only a little older than its most venerable participant. For a third of its existence it was unable to decide just how long it should be.

For all that the marathon has become an international language.

Whether it is as 42.165 kilometres in continental Europe or 26 miles 385 yards in Britain and North America, the marathon now means one thing to everybody — a challenge to triumph over mental doubt and physical frailty.

In a single decade it has grown far beyond the confines of Olympism. Where else in sport can the elite and the ordinary compete together, and both win. Where else in sport can man and woman compete together and, increasingly, on equal terms.

That is the modern marathon, and that is what this book is all about. It is dedicated not to those who will run an Olympic marathon but to those who have never run any marathon, not to those who can conceive of winning but to those who as yet only dream of taking part.

Deliberately we have chosen not to broaden its appeal to those who wish simply to run, whether it is for their own general well-being, as conditioning for another sport or simply for running's own inherent pleasure.

This book is for those for whom the marathon is the appeal, the goal. It may be that you are training towards one already, or that you have run one and would like to run another better. More likely you only dream of running one, and have yet to take the first step along that road.

Whatever your present position, you are in good and growing company. The brotherhood of the marathon, until so recently a closed and exclusive order, is gathering converts daily. In 1970 only 812 Americans ran faster than three hours; in 1975 887 broke through the barrier in a single race. In 1970 the 73-year-old Boston marathon became the first marathon to attract more than 1,000 starters; in 1980 the London marathon was beseiged in its first year with 21,000 who wished to run and a year later with more than 90,000.

In the developed world which demands little physically from its citizens the marathon offers purpose and achievement. As the American running guru Dr George Sheehan put it: 'I believe every human must have the capacity to endure and could find it if he tried. And there is no better place to discover it than in a marathon, for the truth is that every man in a marathon is a survivor or nothing, including the winner.'

How To Use The Book

Chapters 1 and 2, written by Neil Wilson, explore the magic of the marathon, looking at its history and some of the great names associated with the event over the best part of a century. Chapter 2 closes with the arrival of the modern mass marathon, noting that 'It takes all sorts'.

If you want to be among those who enjoy the marathon, Chapter 3 by Andy Etchells looks in detail at how to get kitted out and on the road. The schedule offered here aims to take you to a point where you can comfortably run for 30 minutes at a stretch.

If you are already at this point, you may wish to skip this chapter in preference to the more detailed marathon schedules offered in Chapter 4 by Bruce Tulloh. Plug into any one of the three levels he offers, according to your standard and how long you have been running.

In Chapter 5 Bruce Tulloh discusses the question of routine maintenance for the marathon, offering tips for such things as diet, rest and — whisper it — injury.

By now you'll be thinking about putting your training to the test in a race. Neil Wilson's overview of the marathon year in Chapter 6 should point you in the right direction both in Britain and overseas.

Chapter 7 written by Andy Etchells, suggest strategies for coping with Race Day itself: how to prepare, the kit to take and what to expect when the gun goes off.

Finally, Chapter 8 contains a gallery of profiles of marathoners, both famous and unknown and the last chapter consists of marathon records and statistics and a useful directory of organisations, books and events for your reference.

CHAPTER 1

History and Evolution

MICHEL BREAL was a noted French linguist and historian at the turn of the century. He is not known to have run so much as a metre himself but when the going gets tough and you curse the man who ever thought of marathons, curse him. Breal's brainchild was the marathon.

The legendary run of Philippides, the Greek soldier who usually gets the credit, was no more than a myth with which Breal spiced his creation. Indeed, the only certainty about Philippides is that he never ran a marathon. He died at least 2,300 years too soon.

But let us start at the beginning, not so far back as Ancient Greece and the battlefield of Marathon but in the year of 1895 in the quiet of the Paris study of a 60-year-old Sorbonne professor.

Breal's friend, Baron Pierre de Coubertin, had come up with the splendid notion of re-creating the Olympic Games of Ancient Greece. Breal was a disciple of the cause. He had attended the initial symposium at the Sorbonne in 1892 and the first meeting of the International Olympic Congress which it spawned. He was also an expert on the history of the Ancient Games and was the obvious man to be present in the early planning.

When Coubertin travelled to Athens to meet the local organising committee, Breal accompanied him. The Greeks, sceptical at first because their government was on the verge of bankruptcy and unable to support the project, had been convinced by the enthusiasm of a prominent Athenian writer, Demetrius Vikelas.

Collections among the public had produced vast sums. Millionaire Georgios Averoff, a man in his mid-70s, blessed the scheme with 920,000 drachmae in gold, enough then to reconstruct the Panathenean Stadium in marble. A special stamp issue raised another 400,000 drachmae.

All that had still to be arranged when Coubertin and Breal arrived was the programme. Modern sports were accepted without argument. Curiously all those which had been on the programme at

Ancient Games were rejected. Only the discus, originally an element of the pentathlon, was resurrected as a new event in its own right.

But Breal was convinced that the Games needed more than the discus to capture the hearts of the Greeks. Amid his books in that Paris study the idea came to him. He would create an event to celebrate a Greek legend, the run of Philippides from Marathon to Athens. It was as famous there as Paul Revere's ride was in America or Dick Turpin's in England and was a sure show-stopper.

'If the Organising Committee of the Athens Olympics would be willing to revive the famous run of the Marathon soldier as part of the programme of the Games, I would be glad to offer a prize for this new Marathon race', he wrote to Coubertin, who passed the letter to the Greeks.

They accepted the offer. The prize of a gold cup might have been enough to convince them but their sense of history and national pride made it a certainty. The Greek people were delighted. Distance running had no real tradition there, and certainly not in the Ancient Games but they knew that if Philippides was to be commemorated correctly, a Greek needed to win.

As the legend goes, Philippides was one of the Greek soldiers who, although outnumbered six to one by invading Persians, triumphed on the plain of Marathon under the generalship of Miltiades. Chosen to convey the good news to the elders back in Athens, he ran all the way, greeting them on arrival with the words 'Rejoice, we conquer'. He then dropped dead.

There is not the slightest reason to believe that a word of this is true. None of the contemporary historians gave it book space, and they would never have missed a trick like that. Indeed, it is not until nearly 700 years after the Battle of Marathon that any historian even mentions it.

Herodotus, who is considered the first great historian, was born about the time of the battle, and though he did not write his famous history until late in life, it would have been surprising had he overlooked such current heroics.

Yet Herodotus only mentions Philippides in another context. According to his version he was a runner, a member of the class of Hemerodromoi, an ancient form of dispatch riders. That makes him a professional runner, which Breal and Coubertin were careful to overlook, and, says Herodotus, he was sent from Athens to Sparta to bring help and 'reached Sparta on the very next day after quitting the city of Athens'.

That is a journey of about 140 miles on modern roads, and since much of it would have been on rough, mountainous terrain, that feat alone is extraordinary. Even in 1981, with the aid of modern training techniques and running only on a flat track, the world record for 24 hours was only 169 miles, 705 yards.

Herodotus reports that Philippides returned to Athens with the news that Sparta was unwilling to help, but does not state when. Assuming that he returned as soon as possible that run of around 300 miles was worthy of celebration in its own right.

So where did the story of the Marathon to Athens run appear? Almost certainly in the writings of Plutarch, who, in the first century AD, used the run as a simple scene shifting technique to take his story from Marathon back to the city of Athens.

Certainly it had no influence on the sports-loving Greeks. Distance running was not to their liking, which is hardly surprising in a country so mountainous and so climatically intemperate.

The Ancient Games featured only one event for the first 50 years, the stadium race. This was run around the arena, or a distance of approximately 200 yards. In 724BC a second event, the diaulus, was added; that was merely twice round the arena. Finally, in 720, the dolichus race appeared over a distance of 24 *stadia*, approximately three miles.

Far more famous in reality than Philippides was Leonidas of Rhodes who won all three running events at four consecutive Olympiads over a 12 year period.

But Philippides was legendary. Every Greek knew the story. That was what Breal had suspected, and it proved to be so. In 1896 it became a matter of national pride that the first Olympic marathon should be won by a Greek.

The course followed the traditional route from the village of Marathon, north-east of the capital, past the tomb of the fallen warriors of the Battle of Marathon. The starting point was the bridge at Marathon, the finish in the Olympic Panathenium Stadium. The date was set for April 10, 1896 at 2 pm.

The Greeks went to great lengths to ensure that victory would be theirs. Two preliminary races were held for their own runners over the actual course, the first restricted to members of sports clubs and the second, only a fortnight before the Olympic race, open to all. Twelve contested the first; 38 the second. For both the distance was 40 kilometres, the same intended for the great day and 2,195 metres short of the distance now standard.

It could be said that the first ever winner of a marathon race was Harilaos Vasilakos, winner of that first trial in a time of 3 hours 18 minutes. But though he improved his time by almost 12 minutes one month later in the Olympic race, he was to finish second — and history has never been kind enough to remember Olympic silver medallists.

But the winner of the Olympic title still had to be Greek. There were after all 12 of them in the field of 16, and the four foreigners were hardly prepared for what lay before them. Three had been in action already in the first four days of the Games, Edwin Flack, an Australian working as an accountant in England, winning the 800 and 1,500 metres, American Arthur Blake finishing second in the 1,500 metres and Frenchman Albin Lermusiaux, third.

Flack had run and won the 800 metres the previous day, and that same evening had been transported with the other 15 to Marathon where they spent the night. It was hardly ideal preparation and certainly not to be recommended.

Yet when the gun was fired by a Greek army major the following afternoon, it was the Frenchman who set the pace, and Flack was not far behind him. After 20km they were still there with Blake and the fourth foreigner, Hungarian Gyula Kellner. The leading local was Lavrentis, winner of their second trial race, with Spiridon Louis, who had been fifth in that race, back now in sixth place.

But the steady climb after the flat start was now taking its toll, and runners were beginning to retire. First to go among the leading bunch was Blake at 23km, and a kilometre later Lermusiaux was also in trouble.

Rules were lax for that first marathon, and the runners were permitted assistance. Lermusiaux needed it badly but a thorough rub-down with alcohol soon had him on his feet again, no longer in the lead but at least still in the race.

Ahead was Flack, and the Greeks Harilaos Vasilakos and Louis were challenging. After 32km Lermusiaux finally gave up the struggle and was carried to an accompanying carriage, and at that same point Louis took the lead.

The order now was Louis, Flack, Kellner, Vasilakos and a Greek teenager, Spiridon Belokas, but Flack was flagging, drained by his Olympian efforts of the previous four days. After 37km he collapsed.

Louis now had only to survive to win, and the Greek officer who had started the race and accompanied the runners rode ahead to warn King George I at the stadium that he was about to witness a national triumph.

The stadium was in uproar. A gun, fired when Louis reached the outskirts of Athens, had alerted them and the arrival of the major on his white horse brought the 70,000 crowd to their feet. Finally they saw for themselves the news the King had heard — Louis, a slightly built man, now dust-covered and staggering with exhaustion, was leading into the marble entrance to the stadium.

The King's sons, Crown Prince Nicholas and Prince George, leapt from their seats to run beside Louis to the finishing line. The King waved his naval hat in joy and weeping women threw jewellery at Louis' feet. A full seven minutes behind him came Vasilakos to take second place and behind him a third Greek, Belokas. Fourth was the only foreigner to finish, Kellner.

But Greek pride soon took a fall. Kellner protested that Belokas had never overtaken him, and had to have ridden in a carriage for part of the final stages to have come home third. The Crown

Prince was deputed to investigate, found the claim to be true and stripped Belokas of his placing.

There was no medal for third place at those first Games, and, curiously, the winner received a silver medal instead of the now traditional gold, a diploma and a crown of olive branches.

In the 2 hours 58 minutes 50 seconds it had taken him to run the race, Louis had become a national hero. He also very soon became, like Philippides, a professional under the strict Olympic interpretation. He accepted the gift of an Athens barber of free shaves for life, another gift of free clothing for life and another of 2000lb of chocolate. He was also offered the gift of his choice by the King, and chose a horse and cart.

That was how his secret came out. Louis was not just a peasant farmer. He had been operating a commercial enterprise, transporting fresh water from the wells of his native village of Amaroussion to Athens. He ran beside his old cart all the way there and back, and each day he ran 28km. He was the best prepared man in the race.

Louis was never to run another race but the race he won created interest which spread rapidly across Europe and into North America. Sport had a new event and the world had a new meaning for a word. Marathon was no longer just a race of abnormal length. It now meant a test of extreme endurance, and there were many runners eager to accept the challenge.

The Americans were the next to call their race a marathon although there had been races of around 40km even before the first Olympics. Kellner, who finished third in Athens, had qualified by winning a trial of that distance in Hungary. But the Americans who had been in Athens saw an intriguing connection. Many of them were from Boston where the local Athletic Association was well organised. If Athens could commemorate Philippides' run, why should Boston not mark the heroic ride of Paul Revere.

They decided the following year on Patriot's Day, April 19, itself a public holiday, they would organise a race on a course resembling that in Athens. It should have been the first in the world outside Greece but in the end it was not even the first in America. On September 20, 1896, just five months after the Olympic marathon, the New York City Knickerbocker Athletic Club introduced one into their regular athletic meeting.

Twenty-five miles from New York in Stamford, Connecticut, 30 runners began just before lunch-time through roads heavy with mud from the morning's rain. It was a hilly course, too, and John McDermott's winning time was, not surprisingly, almost half an hour slower than Louis' in Athens.

However, the crowd's reaction was significant. Many had gathered at the Columbia Oval for the athletics meeting but the reporter of the *New York Times* claimed that when McDermott appeared in the stadium for the final lap judges stopped their work; athletes found time to become spectators.

There was, he wrote, 'a pandemonium of joy. Women who knew only that the first race of its kind ever held in this country was nearing a finish waved their handkerchiefs and fairly screamed with excitement. Men dashed from their seats. . .'

Ten runners finished, the crowd apparently yelled itself hoarse, and it must have been obvious to anybody there that this was an event to grip the public imagination. It was to be the same at Boston the following April.

The *Boston Daily Globe* reported that so great was the number of carriages and wagons attempting to follow the runners leaving the road outside Metcalfe's mill in Ashland that 'there was hardly room to turn around'.

Again it was McDermott, the winner in New York, who led the way for much of the distance. He took the lead from Hamilton Gray, who had finished second to him in New York, and for the first 20 miles his main problem was the vast crowd. His attendants had to work hard to keep the road clear ahead of him.

He slowed to a walk there, and when he resumed running was halted by a leg cramp. Vigorous rubbing of the leg eased the trouble, and although he was forced to walk again before the finish he still won by almost seven minutes. Five of the first six were New Yorkers, and they were as dominant at Boston for the next two stagings of the race.

There are few records now of the training programmes of these early pioneers. Newspapers of the time reported that the winner of the third Boston, Lawrence Brignolia, prepared for the first Boston with a few days training and a heavy meal! Incredibly, he finished that year but it must have been as a result of the stamina gained in his main sport of rowing. A year later when he devoted 'a whole month' to preparing himself he improved his time by more than an hour to finish fifth, and in 1899 he became the only man to have finished all three Bostons when he won. Again he improved his time despite losing five minutes because of a heavy fall.

The chief disadvantage runners of the time suffered was in their equipment. It was the belief then that the body had to be kept warm to survive a marathon. So even in warm weather, runners were clad in half-sleeved shirts and knee-length shorts and in cooler conditions some wore full-length worsted tights. There was also a claim that gained credence among runners that nothing should be drunk during the race, with the possible exception of beef tea. Joe Forshaw, bronze medallist in the 1908 Olympics, wrote a year later: 'I know from actual experience that the full race can be covered in creditable time without so much as a single drop of water being taken or even sponging of the head.'

Today, of course, more than 80 years of trial and error has shown that far less clothing need be worn and regular drinks en route are advisable if not essential. The world's fastest-ever marathoner, Derek Clayton, says that he did not take fluid during his two fastest races but dehydration from sweating raises the body's temperature and is a crucial contributory factor towards heat stroke. So most top runners drink regularly.

Recent scientific investigation has shown that a fluid loss of more than three per cent of the total body weight causes dehydration, and since it is possible to lose up to two litres of sweat an hour running in warm weather, drinking is necessary to make it up.

The early marathoners, of course, did not have the advantage of any medical or scientific advice. The first known manual on marathon running was not published in America until 1909, and while that contained the framework of preparations still recommended today, there were some howlers.

Nor did they have the other advantage of custom-built shoes. No company in those days made a shoe specifically for running on roads, and most marathoners converted the black leather lightweight shoes made for cyclists.

Considering all these handicaps it is amazing that times were so good. They are difficult to compare with modern races because no races then were as long as today, most aiming for around 40km with some like the Boston measured at around 24¾ miles. But in 1907, only 11 years, remember, since the first marathon, Thomas Longboat, a Canadian Indian teenager, won the Boston at a pace faster than six-minute miling. It was so good that it would still have won him the Olympic title in 1948!

The Boston was a well-organised race, controlled by experienced athletics officials, but few other races at the turn of the century enjoyed such good order. The 1900 Olympic marathon was an example of the worse kind, an extreme example perhaps but typical of some.

That second Olympics was a shambles in all respects. The Olympic founder Coubertin is alleged to have confided to friends that he never understood how his ideal survived its second celebration.

Paris did not want the event, and it was spread across several months at venues throughout the city. Competitors missed finals because of sudden programme changes, finished by fighting each other and at least one man died 68 years later believing himself to be a silver medallist when he had in fact been eliminated in a semi-final.

The marathon was typical of the entire affair. It was not even called the Olympic marathon, Parisian newspapers referred to it as the Tour de Paris. Not surprisingly, the winner, a French baker's roundsman, Michel Theato, did not learn until twelve years later that he had become an official Olympic champion!

Theato recalled when told he was an Olympic champion that he had run in a race around Paris in 1900 in suffocating heat — the temperature was reported to be 102F (39C) — and had finished in 2hrs 59min 45sec. The laurels that won him were a surprise to him.

There were only eight finishers in the race, four of them Americans. One of those, Dick Grant, tried unsuccessfully to sue the International Olympic Committee — he at least must have known whose race he was running in — claiming that a cyclist had knocked him down as he was about to overtake Theato. The cyclist was part of a plot to ensure France's only athletics winner, he argued. The Court did not agree.

Marathons were springing up everywhere now. Belgium staged a national championship, the Austrians hosted a race won by

Czechs and the Swiss held their first championship. In North America Canadians dominated at Boston, and crowds were drawn everywhere to the magic of the marathon.

Unfortunately the race attracted more than its reasonable share of controversy. The 1904 Olympic was no exception. The characters competing were curious enough. Two were South African Kaffir tribesmen who happened to be working at the World Exposition then being held in St Louis. Another was a five foot tall Cuban postman, Felix Carvajal, who claimed he had run the island's length carrying mail.

Again, as in Paris, the temperature was far too hot, around 90F (32C), the roads were largely unpaved and dusty, there were several hills and water only at a well after 12 miles. The suffering of the runners was appalling. One, a Californian called Garcia, had to be rushed to hospital after inhaling too much dust, and nearly died.

Carvajal, incredibly, had turned up in a long sleeved shirt, long trousers, heavy street shoes and a beret. A spectator shortened the trousers with scissors but attired so unsuitably he still managed to survive to finish fourth.

The real controversy surrounded New Yorker Fred Lorz, an experienced marathoner. He had led the race in its early stages but after nine miles he retired with cramp, and was picked up by a truck.

For more than 10 miles he rode in style until the truck itself broke down. Recovered by then, he decided to run the rest of the way to the stadium and, for a joke, run into the stadium. Some joke! It must have broken the leader Tom Hicks' heart when Lorz casually overtook him looking fresh and untroubled. He even took the final two hills easily.

Hicks, on the other hand, had almost collapsed with 10 miles to go, was refused a drink by his helpers and not allowed to lie down for a rest. Ashen-faced, he was barely moving when Lorz streaked past him.

But Lorz took the joke too far. He entered the stadium looking cooler than the spectators, was acclaimed and photographed with Alice Roosevelt, daughter of the American President.

Fifteen minutes later Hicks arrived, staggering, but when the results were announced the timekeepers and judges who had accompanied Hicks all the way and knew he was the winner, turned on Lorz. He was disqualified from the race and struck off the race results. Within days the Amateur Athletic Union, the governing body of athletics in America whose secretary-general James Sullivan happened to be the Games Director, had suspended Lorz for life from amateur athletics.

Life turned out to be only eight months because when Lorz was allowed time to explain the joke, officials saw the funny side. He had not intended to hoodwink anybody, he said, and was baffled by the ceremony surrounding him when he reached the stadium. So they lifted his suspension and in his very next race in Boston he won fairly and squarely.

Hicks was less fortunate. The only English-born runner ever to win an Olympic marathon, he was so badly scarred mentally and physically by the ordeal that he never ran one again.

What is interesting now when no assistance may be given to marathoners beyond that available to all at the drinks stations was how much help Hicks had been given. A tank of water had been kept warm on an accompanying steam-driven car and Hicks was bathed in it regularly. He was refused drinking water but his mouth was sponged out with distilled water, and after 18 miles he was given 1/60th grain of strychnine sulphate, a nervous system stimulant now banned by the International Amateur Athletic Federation. The strychnine was mixed with egg white, and was given at least twice during the race. He also received egg white on its own and at least one sip of brandy!

How uneducated were runners then in the modern techniques of distance running can be gauged from the Cuban Carjaval's experience. He stopped en route to eat green fruit from a roadside bush. Not surprisingly, he was seized by stomach cramps later in the race. Mind you, Spiridon Louis drank plentiful quantities of wine during the first Olympic marathon, and that did him no harm.

Again in 1908, when the Olympics moved to London, the marathon encountered problems. In what was to become the most famous marathon of all time, warmth and humidity again turned the race into a desperate struggle for survival for at least one man, the leader Dorando Pietri.

He had failed to finish in the Intermediary Games in Athens two years earlier but he was an experienced and successful runner, and it was no surprise that he figured so well throughout the race.

This time the runners created their own difficulties with a pace as hot as the day. The Briton Jack Price took the field of 56 through the first three miles at a near five minute mile pace. Another Briton, Fred Lord, took up the challenge and maintained the pace until 10 miles when his compatriot pulled away. The British seemed determined to impress in their capital city but they had misjudged the day.

After 15 miles Price was out of the race, the other Britons were all well back and a South African Charles Heffron was ahead. But all this time, keeping well up with the leaders, was the Italian Pietri. At 20 miles he was almost four minutes behind Heffron, at 22 miles only 2½ minutes and at 24 miles two minutes. With a mile to go he was ahead.

Unfortunately for the Italian the British had chosen this fourth Olympic marathon to raise the distance to 26 miles 385 yards, a length arrived at to suit the Royal Family. They had wanted to see the start from Windsor Castle windows and, naturally, the finish had to be in front of the Royal Box at the White City. That meant the 26 miles they had intended only took the course to the entrance of the stadium. So 385 yards were added (the City track was nearly 600 yards (536 metres) in circumference). It was that 385 yards which literally floored Pietri.

Coming down the ramp from the road to the cinder track, he became disorientated, and fell in front of the main stand.

People rushed to his aid. He was lifted to his feet, and began running unsteadily. Twice more on the single bend he had to negotiate he fell. He was sponged down but fell again coming into the final straight. Virtually on the finish line he collapsed, falling this time into the arms of Jack Andrew, secretary of Polytechnic Harriers, the club entrusted with the race organisation.

Pietri had crossed the finishing line but was disqualified for receiving assistance on the line. Andrew was unrepentant. He had, he said, acted on the race doctor's orders. Clearly, the Italian should have been removed from the track after his first fall and saved any further distress. As it was, he was close to death for the next two and a half hours.

The race went instead to John Hayes, of America, who had

finished half a minute later, and two more Americans were third and fourth. Sensibly they had never followed the suicidal pace set by the Britons, who finished back in twelfth place and beyond.

Hayes was promoted by his New York store on his return, and soon cashed in on a boom in marathon interest there by turning professional as a runner. But the race will always be remembered as Dorando's marathon, and when he had recovered, Queen Alexandra, at the prompting of Sherlock Holmes' creator, Sir Arthur Conan Doyle, presented him with a large gold cup that was a replica of the one awarded to Hayes.

The inscription read: 'To Pietri Dorando in Remembrance of the Marathon Race From Windsor to the Stadium July 24, 1908 from Queen Alexandra'. The pity was that, like the start list, the inscribers had his names reversed. Not that this handicapped him; he turned professional, like Hayes, and forever more was known simply as Dorando.

The race had captured the public imagination. Suddenly entrepreneurs in America realised the potential. Hayes was persuaded to meet Dorando again for money. So was the Canadian Indian Longboat, who had finished his amateur career failing to finish in the Olympics. They were joined, too, by Briton Alfred Shrubb, holder of world records at four distances.

The race everybody wanted was the re-match of Hayes with Dorando. It happened that November indoors in Madison Square Gardens with the unfortunate runners expected to circle a wooden track 260 times. Dorando won by about 80 yards. Three weeks later he ran again, this time against Longboat and again at the Garden. Each man received $3,750. Dorando collapsed within the last mile, and again had to be carried off, and when he challenged Longboat again the following month was forced to retire. Incredibly he came back twice that month to win other professional races.

The money being offered for Hayes, Dorando and the others was enormous. And so demanding did the public become that on one day in May 1909 three marathons were run in New York alone. One produced a fastest time ever by an amateur. But the big one was billed as the Marathon Derby at the New York Polo Grounds. It was the second Derby, and like the first the purse was $10,000, 5,000 to go to the winner.

The first had been scheduled as another Dorando versus Hayes race but an unknown French restauranteur, Henri St Yves, who was only five feet tall, had intervened and won it with Dorando second and Hayes third. The second brought another easy win for St Yves, the only difference being that his odds in the stadium had been slashed from 40-1 to 2-1.

Promoters and gamblers were turning the Olympic race classic into a circus. In the second Marathon Derby one runner was forced back on the track so often by his backers that he eventually fell unconscious and did not recover consciousness for ten minutes. The money men did not care how they staged a race as long as there was a crowd to see it. In England one organiser persuaded Dorando to race local opposition round and round the Royal Albert Hall on coconut matting. Every mile needed 20 laps. Even the amateur organisers were finding unusual venues. One race was run round the decks of the warship *Wyoming* in San Francisco harbour. The race needed 355 laps and only two finished.

But the publicity generated by the one-off events was popularising the event. More runners wanted to participate. Fields were often now above 100. In London in 1909 a race which exists to this day, the Polytechnic Harriers Marathon, was run for the first time, organised by the club which had been responsible for the previous year's Olympic race and starting in the same place at Windsor Park. It finished that year at Stamford Bridge, in Chelsea, briefly transferred to the White City in the 1930s and later to Chiswick but now confines itself to local roads around Windsor.

That first race was won by Poly club member Harry Barret in a world best time of 2 hours, 42 minutes, 31 seconds but a year later at Boston a Canadian, Fred Cameron, running his first marathon, beat another debutante Clarence DeMar in a far more significant race.

DeMar was to dominate marathon running for the next 20 years. Eventually he was dubbed Mr Marathon. But it was his final triumph over those who campaigned against ultra-distance running as a danger to health which was so important to the long term future of the marathon.

DeMar came from a poor Ohio family of six and was forced to leave university to support his mother. But he had taken up running while there, and after running 26 miles in a training session entered that 1910 Boston. A year later, watched by a crowd of 200,000, he won in 2:21:39.6, a course record. Few of those spectators could have known that DeMar had a heart murmur, discovered shortly before the race.

In 1912 DeMar stopped racing, concerned about the threat to his suspect heart. It was not until 1917 that he ran the Boston again. He finished third, and finally in 1921, by which time he was married and at the age of 33 had started a large family, he resumed seriously.

Then it was by chance. A sleet storm forced him to run to and from work. His work-mates encouraged him to train again. Soon he had pushed his training back to 100 miles a week, and in the next nine years he was to win the Boston six more times, and win a bronze medal at the 1924 Olympics.

During this time DeMar became one of the first guinea pigs of the Harvard Fatigue Laboratory where it was discovered in treadmill and bicycle tests that far from having a heart problem, DeMar had incredible cardiovascular stamina. He was to continue to run marathons until he was 66 by which time he had finished more than 100. It was obvious that those who ran not only suffered no ill effects but benefited. The marathon was not the killer some had claimed and many had suspected after Dorando's race.

There were those who died but they were so exceptional as to be notable. One died in the 1912 Olympic marathon, a race like all previous Olympic marathons run in high temperatures.

He was Francisco Lazaro, a 21-year-old Portuguese who collapsed in the sweltering heat and died the following day. It was never revealed whether the heat alone or a heart condition had caused his death.

Stockholm could not be criticised for its organisation. Certainly that was not a contributory factor in Lazaro's case. For the first time there were regular refreshment and watering points. Indeed it was at one drinks stand that the race was decided.

Two South Africans were running together near the stadium. One, Christian Gitsham, stopped for a drink; the other, Kenneth McArthur continued. Gitsham never recovered his rhythm, and lost by a little less than a minute. Many finished in poor condition, a 17-year-old Italian Carlo Speroni collapsed within sight of the finish and half the field failed to finish. But 17 finished in under three hours, and McArthur's pace was the fastest to win an Olympic marathon.

The Twenties saw the marathon mature into a specialised distance, more rigidly regulated and controlled. Gone now were attendants and coaches, professionalism of the pre-war years had all but died out and the race developed its own great heroes, legends such as the Finn Hannes Kolehmainen, the first of the great Britons Sam Ferris, America's Albert Michelsen and DeMar.

More significantly it was finally awarded its own distance. Today nobody is sure why the International Olympic Committee decided that the 1908 'bastard' distance of 26 miles 385 yards (or 42,195 metres) should forever more be the standard Olympic marathon distance. It was the least logical of all distances since it had been arrived at for no better reason than to keep a Queen and her family happy. Far more logical for an organisation such as the IOC, which had its headquarters in metric Switzerland, would have been 40 kilometres.

For whatever reason then, the IOC dictated that from the 1924 Games in Paris the 'English' distance would be standard, and gradually other major races fell into line. Boston changed in 1927 and the New York Yonkers race, an annual event since 1907, switched in 1935. Only the Poly Marathon had been the correct distance since its conception in 1909, and it was not until 1972 when the directing vehicle led the runners astray that the Poly organisers had a non-standard distance event.

The last of the odd-length Olympic races was in Antwerp in 1920, and that was the only Olympic race ever to be longer than standard, an extra 555 metres. It was also the first Olympic race in which runners averaged better than six minute miling, and all three medallists achieved it.

The winner was Hannes Kolehmainen, one of three brothers from the town of Kuopio, in the Finnish lake district. He had run his first marathon in 1907 at the age of 17 but concentrated more on track racing. He set world records for 2000 and 3000 metres, and at the 1912 Olympics won the 5000 in a world record time, the 10,000 and the now-defunct 8000 metres cross country.

He then emigrated to America and for several years disappeared from athletics. Only the lure of another Olympics in 1920, by which time he was 30, made him resume training. He won the American Olympic marathon trial, and the Finns chose him for their team. And what a team! It was to take four of the first 10 places in Antwerp with Hannes winning a remarkable battle with Estonian Juri Lossmann. His winning margin of 13 seconds was the closest Olympic marathon ever.

The Finns set the pace throughout the 1920s. Another of their countrymen, Albin Stenroos, won the 1924 Olympic title and Finns took the bronze medals in the 1928 and 1932 Games. Much of the credit went to their national coach Lauri Pinkala but several of the Finns swore by walking as the basis of their phenomenal endurance. Several claimed to walk about 60 kilometres weekly and run as far again.

The marathon was a race for all nationalities. The 1928 Olympic was won by Boughera El Ouafi. He ran in the colours of France but he was an Algerian born and bred, the first African to win an Olympic title. The 1932 gold medal went to an Argentinian, Juan Carlos Zabala.

Zabala had been discovered by a Scottish physical educationist

Andrew Stirling when he was 13. He was an orphan and Stirling befriended him, teaching him to train and steering him to the South American continental 10,000 metres title at the age of 20. A year later Stirling took his protégé to Europe to prepare for that year's Olympics. He promptly set a new world 30km record, won the famous Kosice race in his marathon debut and in that race became the fourth fastest ever on an out-and-back course.

Ironically, Stirling's careful coaching led Zabala to beat Briton Sam Ferris for the gold medal. There was just 19 seconds between them at the finish, and for the first time in an Olympic marathon, the first four finishers were so close that they were all on the stadium track simultaneously.

Zabala collapsed at the finish; Ferris, who was a few days short of his 32nd birthday, finished fresh. So why had he not made his effort sooner? Years later he was to reveal the reason. On a training run over the Olympic course, he had spotted a large hoarding advertising milk one mile from the finish. He stored that information away in his mind as a marker for where he should start his final surge. But on race day Ferris never saw the hoarding. It had been obscured by a temporary viewing stand.

Ferris' magnificent career ended the following year when he won his eighth Polytechnic marathon. It was his 12th win in 19 starts, and he had been runner-up in another four. In an age when the world best was barely 2½ hours, he had run 10 marathons faster than 2hrs 40min, and none slower than 2hrs 54mins.

Britain was second again at the 1936 Olympics in Berlin. This time their Ernie Harper ran the fastest marathon of his life to win the silver behind the first Japanese winner of the Olympic title, Kitei Son. Son was in fact Korean, a country then annexed by the Japanese, and it is one of the curiosities of Olympic marathons that not one native of Japan has won the title in spite of the event's mammoth popularity there.

More intriguing was Son's age. He was 21, and yet his win in Berlin was to be his last marathon. He was a track runner, specialising in shorter distances who was converted for the purpose of the Olympics only. He had previously been better known for distances between 1500 and 5000 metres, and was perhaps the forerunner of the present generation of star marathoners who are so often successful at shorter track distances before they move to the marathon.

It was interesting, too, that the Japanese were then so young while the best Britons were all peaking later. Harper was 34, Ferris in 1932 had been 32, Bert Norris, another Britain in Berlin, was 37 and Dunky Wright, a Briton fourth in the 1932 Olympics, had then been 36. Squire Yarrow, later to become president of the Amateur Athletic Association and a silver medallist in the 1938 European marathon championship, was 33 when he ran his debut race.

The same was true of the Briton after World War II. The first AAA Championship after the war was won by Yarrow, by then 41, with Duncan Robertson second at the age of 41 and Dunky Wright fifth at 51! The 1947 title went to Jack Holden, then 40, whose fame had been won pre-war when he took the International Cross Country Championship four times.

His incredible second life as an athlete climaxed in 1950 when he won the Empire, Midland, AAA, Polytechnic and European titles. Not even the blisters which forced him to run the last eight miles barefoot or the Great Dane which attacked him in the last two miles could stop him winning the Empire race. 'I was just glad the dog didn't fancy English meat,' said Holden, who was himself a dog lover and a breeder of Staffordshire terriers.

Elsewhere younger men were dominating. A 19-year-old Korean, Kee Yong Ham, who was coached by 1936 Olympic champion Kitei Son, won the Boston in 1950, a 19-year-old American John Kelley won the New York Yonkers race and to complete the trio Japan sent 19-year-old Shigeki Tanaka to win the 1951 Boston.

But the first great hero of the 1950s was an older man, Emile Zatopek, a son of a Czechoslovakian carpenter who was only two months short of his 30th birthday at the 1952 Helsinki Olympics.

Zatopek was an awkward, little man, who ran with hunched shoulders and a style which had never been recommended by any textbook. But he won the 10,000 metres Olympic title in 1948 and the 5000 and 10,000 metres in Helsinki. If that was not enough he had also entered the marathon in Helsinki, an incomprehensible decision since he had never run so far in his life, would have only two days rest after the 5000 metres final and would have run more than 12 miles of Olympic heats and finals before it.

But Zatopek was a phenomenal trainer. He had run for miles in mid-winter in army boots. He invented an exercise of bounding with high knee lifts through thick snow. He trained with weights. Most important of all, he employed 'interval training', repeated fast runs to build up speed interspersed with jogging to build endurance. In 1948 he was running as many as sixty 400 metres in a single day with only 200 metres jogging between each.

But he had not run further than a half-marathon, and in that Helsinki field was the Briton, Jim Peters, 33 years old but the world's fastest ever marathoner. It was a duel between them Peters led for 10 miles until Zatopek caught him. With the Swede Gustaf Jansson, they ran as a group for two miles.

Zatopek was now beyond anything he had ever run, and yet, coming to Peters' shoulder, he asked: 'Can't you go any faster?'

Peters recalls: 'I told him I could although my legs were beginning to pain me considerably. Zatopek just shrugged his shoulders and forged 200 yards ahead and looked round to see if I was following him'.

Peters did not follow for much longer. After 20 miles he was attacked by cramp. Sam Ferris, who was a spectator at that point, encouraged him to start again but 200 metres later Peters was forced to retire.

Zatopek, meanwhile, chatted with anybody who would listen and never again lost the lead. He won in a time which improved the Olympic record by 6min 16secs.

Peters could reasonably blame his trip to Helsinki for his retirement. He had been flown there in an ex-wartime transport plane, with temporary seating and a howling wind blowing straight along the length of the plane. There was no food and no hot drinks, and because of appalling weather the flight lasted nine hours.

Peters had retired from athletics in 1948 but had been persuaded by his trainer Johnny Johnston to return to try the marathon. He had set a British record in his debut, and in 1953 and 1954 set four world records for the marathon. Indeed, he transformed the event, becoming the first man to run below 2hrs 20 minutes and doing it four times before any other runner managed it.

Peters, unfortunately, will always be remembered for one disastrous race, the 1954 Empire Games marathon in Vancouver. He had won the bronze medal in the six miles in the Games' first week. Now he faced the marathon against a background of a cloudless sky, temperatures around 80F and a noon start.

It was a foolish decision to schedule a marathon to start at noon in early August, and the runners paid for official stupidity. Peters did not help his own cause by the pace he set, fast enough for most of the race to finish in 2hrs 20mins. His friend Stan Cox who kept closest to him was so badly affected by the heat that he ran into a telegraph pole after 24 miles and had to retire.

Peters himself began to wobble on the hill leading to the stadium. As he ran onto the track, he fell. He got up, lurched to one side and fell again. There were only 380 yards to the finish but he fell a dozen times on the way to it. 'I thought I had fallen three times but I learned later it was far more often,' says Peters. 'The few yards that I covered took me as long as running two miles would normally'.

The finish line edged slowly, agonisingly closer. His English team-mates, still hoarse from cheering Roger Bannister to victory in the Miracle Mile that afternoon, roared at him from the trackside to continue. Each step they followed him, banging the ground to alert him when he fell.

Finally he reached the finishing line, falling into the arms of Mick Mayes, the British team masseur. But it was not the finishing line for the marathon. Peters had not made it. Like Dorando, he was disqualified for receiving assistance.

Now the fight to save his life would begin.

John Savidge, the English shot putter, lifted him in his arms and rushed him to a stretcher. In the dressing room he regained conciousness momentarily. 'A nurse was bending over me,' he recalls. '"Did I win?" I asked her. She smiled at me. "You did very well," she said.' Peters spent the next two days fighting for his life, much of the time in an oxygen tent.

Meanwhile legend was being created behind him. A Vancouver reporter claimed that the Scot Joe McGhee was sitting in a ditch, waiting for an ambulance to take him away when he heard that Peters and Cox were out of the race. Exhorted by a Scottish lady to continue for the honour of Scotland, he waved away the ambulance and ran on to victory.

So many believed this story that it was reported as fact in a British newspaper and subsequently appeared in the official history of the Amateur Athletic Association. But it was only fantasy.

McGhee refused to become embroiled in the 'ballyhoo', as he calls it, and he did not seek to put the record straight for a quarter of a century. But angered by the 'shockingly untrue' report in the AAA report, he has now given his own version.

'At no time did I collapse,' he says. 'On one occasion only, I tripped momentarily on the kerb. Indeed over the last four miles I was engaged in a very active race pulling away from two South Africans, Jackie Mekler and Johann Barnard, who had come close at 22 miles. I never knew I was first until I was near the stadium and, indeed, at that time I was absolutely delighted to be finishing second'.

Unfortunately for McGhee, and for Hayes who won the 1908 Olympic race, nobody today remembers their victories. The 1908 race is the Dorando affair; the 1954 race the Peters' marathon. Legend has clouded the facts.

Surely, though, the occasional failure of great runners like these is part of the magic of the marathon. If Everest were as easy as climbing a ladder, who would be interested in the climb?

CHAPTER 2

The Seventies Boom

NOTHING SO FAR in the evolution of the marathon gave us reason to believe that the event was anything more than an esoteric activity of an athletic fringe. Few wished to participate and there were comparatively few competitions. In the whole of the United States as recently as 1969 fewer than 50 were run; in Britain until far more recently as few as a dozen.

For most the marathon came alive every four years at the Olympics. Interest in other major races was more localised. The spectators admired and respected those who ran; they did not seek to emulate. The marathon was still something for the super-human, not for the likes of everyday man, and certainly not for a lady.

Abebe Bikila's performance in winning the 1960 Rome Olympic race was greeted typically. Here was a man from a primitive African country running the fastest Olympic marathon of all time round the streets of Rome in his bare feet! It was extraordinary but it was not a feat that prompted many to rush out to try for themselves. Not like Olga Korbutt's gymnastics did in 1972.

Fields everywhere were relatively small. The Boston, the largest, was surprised when 227 started in 1963. The previous year's European championship race had attracted only 14 countries. Few fields exceeded a hundred. Only slowly towards the end of the 1960s did numbers creep higher, and then only in the United States.

In Britain, in 1973, there was the ultimate proof in Ian Thompson that runners who had never succeeded on the track beyond the standard of their own club could achieve spectacular results in the marathon. Ian Thompson was not an instant success, he had been a runner for 10 years before he ran his first marathon. But he had never been more than competent on the track.

Then he was persuaded to run in the AAA marathon at Harlow because his club at Luton needed an extra runner to enter the team event. He was at best a 30min 10sec 10,000 metres runner, 'a grafter rather than a genius,' as he puts it. When he came home as the new AAA champion, complete with a prize of a power drill and a ticket to the Commonwealth Games, even his brother refused to believe him. 'He rang around among our friends to check my story,' says Ian.

Ian, of course, went on to win that Commonwealth title, and the European title and run the fastest time by any Briton. He was the rabbit who became a star, and there must have been a million Walter Mittys with visions less fantastic that what Thompson proved was possible. Yet few were prompted to give it a try.

What happened since owes everything to North America but in the decade after Bikila's first Olympic victory the marathon hardly excited that success-concious nation. It was nine years after Peters had breeched the 2:20 barrier before an American followed him, and then it was Buddy Edelen who had been living and training in Britain. For 11 years Americans could not even win their own classic race at Boston. No American had won the Olympic title since 1904 if you exclude Hayes' 1908 elevation after the disqualification of Pietri.

Then it happened. With the Seventies dawned a dramatic and novel interest in running. Initially, it was called jogging, a slower, more relaxed and non-competitive style of running which the athletic fraternity dismissed as a sideshow. Then regular joggers began to enter marathons, and finish. Women, too. Suddenly thousands wanted to prove that they could do it. The marathon became the challenge, not of a single generation but of every generation of a single country. Even a four-year-old ran it!

But why? What had sparked off the enthusiasm for running 26 miles 385 yards, or 26.2 as the American came to call it. Why were there only 44 marathons in the United States in 1969 and more than 130 by 1974?

Standards rose tremendously. In 1970 around 700 Americans ran faster than three hours. Three years later more than twice as many did. Starting numbers doubled, trebled and finally soared. Nearly six times as many ran Boston in 1974 as 10 years earlier. By 1978 Boston was overwhelmed with almost 4,500 starters and another 2,000 unofficial runners. And in that race more than 92 per cent finished under four hours!

Where did these legions come from, and what Pied Piper were they following? Many commentators suggest it was Frank Shorter, the American who won the 1972 Olympic marathon in Munich.

That was a bad Olympics for America's athletes. Shorter's victory, the first by an American marathoner since 1908, was all the more welcome, and satellite television which networked his triumph made him an instant hero. He had the right image, too, as his subsequent advertising contracts were to prove.

But it is more probable that Shorter caught an existing mood. The number of marathons had doubled between 1969 and 1970 when Shorter was still a little known track runner. In the months of 1972 before he won the Olympic title there had been several marathons with more than 200 finishers.

Americans had become a sedentary people in the 1950s. Television had confined them to their armchairs. In the 1960s they were busy demonstrating, marching and protesting against Vietnam, or for other civil rights issues.

Slowly but surely the most technologically-advanced nation in the world returned to nature. Initially it was only the hippies, flower people and surfers but ultimately it was middle America, back-packing, camping, climbing and searching for new frontiers.

Health became a topic of concern. Track coaches, Arthur Lydiard in New Zealand and Bill Bowerman at the University of Oregon, spread the word of the benefits of jogging. Then Kenneth Cooper, a consultant on physical fitness to the United States Air Force, wrote a book called *Aerobics*, followed by *The New Aerobics* and with his wife, *Aerobics for Women*.

Cooper's theory was that for exercise to be an effective contribution to health it had to improve cardiovascular fitness, to benefit heart, circulation and respiration. He pointed out that this could only happen with sustained exercise. He suggested not less than 15 minutes, and argued that most sports simply did not qualify. Tennis, golf, soccer and the more traditional games had too many stops and starts. Running, brisk walking, swimming and cycling were to be recommended.

The endorsement of the American Heart Association and the President's Council on Physical Fitness and Sports for jogging furthered the campaign, and there were calculable indications in the

Seventies that heart disease was declining among Americans but increasing still among the more sedentary Europeans.

There were detractors. The top American newspaper columnist William F. Buckley pointed out that dying of a heart attack was often painless and swift but were the alternatives 'cancer, leprosy and Creutzfeldt-Jakob disease?' It was, he suggested, 'a question to consider during those hours we do not spend jogging'. But his was a voice in the wilderness.

Curiously, America, the land of the competitor and the winner, was seized with the revolutionary concept of simple participation. To thousands it no longer mattered whether they beat others only, that they challenged themselves to live a more Spartan life. Losing became respectable; success was measured in participation alone. It was the original Olympic ideal re-discovered.

There were other contributory reasons. The advent of inner city marathons which garnered enormous media attention created its own momentum. The New York City Marathon, organised by the New York Road Runners Club, attracted 126 runners in 1970. For five years it was run around a boring five lap circuit of Central Park. In 1975 it still had only 275 finishers. In 1976 it was switched to a point-to-point course through five of New York's city boroughs on a Sunday morning to help celebrate the United States Bicentennial — and 2,000 runners turned up, an incredible rise in one year. By 1981 there were 16,000 starters and another 30,000 who wished to run but had to be refused. More than two million turned out to watch.

It was the same in Chicago. In 1977 5,000 runners; a year later, 10,000. In Boston numbers became so great that for the first time organisers imposed a qualifying standard of 3 hours for men and 3¼ hours for women and veterans. In 1979 there were enough qualified to extend the starting list to 8,000, and local police estimated another 3,000 gatecrashed the race. By the end of the decade Americans had the option of almost 300 marathons.

Health was the rallying cry. Lose weight, lower blood pressure, prolong life, broadcast the devotees. And the campaign became a crusade, its high priests men such as Dr Cooper, George Sheehan and James E. Fixx.

Here was another curiosity. To triumph like Shorter, who almost repeated his Olympic win four years later when he won the silver medal, or Bill Rodgers, the Bostonian who kept winning the Boston in the late Seventies, was not part of the game. Emulation, so much part of competitive sports, was hardly noticeable.

The gurus were the doctors, the writers and those who had been runners themselves. Fixx claimed to be nearly 16 stone and struggling to run 50 yards when he took up running. It was only an injury sustained playing tennis that started him. He wanted to improve his fitness for tennis, started running, gave up smoking and suddenly found himself a new addiction.

Fixx wrote about his experiences and those of friends and acquaintances in *The Complete Book of Running*. For 18 months the book was in the American list of bestsellers. In that time it sold 750,000 in hardback. If anybody needed proof that something phenomenal was happening that was it.

There was another factor — women. For most of the century they had been positively discouraged. When they began in the late Sixties proving that not only could they survive the test of 26.2 miles but could run it as fast as most men, the marathon lost much of its element of fear. Peters and Dorando were forgotten; if a teenage girl could run it faster than three hours, what man was there who didn't think he could do so too.

There is some evidence that the first woman to complete a marathon was a Greek girl, Melopene. She was refused permission to run in the first Olympic marathon but there have been reports that she ran behind the men, finishing in about 4½ hours.

More certainly, a British woman, Violet Piercy, ran over the Poly marathon course in 1926, finishing in 3hrs 40mins 22secs. But that was not a race. She ran alone, and none sought to emulate her achievement until 1963 when Merry Lepper timed 3:37:03 in Culver City. A few months later in Britain Dale Greig bettered that by nearly 10 minutes, running unofficially in a race in the Isle of Wight.

All of these successes were unofficial. Nowhere were women permitted to take part in distance running. The British had proposed the inclusion of a women's 800 metres in the 1928 Olympics with unfortunate results. Several of the under-trained ladies failed to finish and some who did were distressed. It was another 36 years before the International Olympic Committee was prepared to try again, and not until 1972 that they dared go so far as allowing women to run as far as 1,500 metres.

It was a traditionalist's attitude. Women had been barred for religious reasons on pain of death from so much as watching the Ancient Olympics. The IOC's concern was with their health but physical rather than spiritual. Old wives' tales abounded. Women were more prone to injury; fertility was impaired; they lost femininity and became muscular. More probably their exclusion was the result of male pride.

Women's Liberation, the movement which spread so fast and effectively in the Sixties and Seventies, was determined to put an end to athletic discrimination. Anything men could do, they at least wanted to try. Physiologists supported their case. The longer the distance the more even the balance between the sexes, they argued. Men's greater physical strength was not a significant advantage over the longer distances of running.

The active suffragettes were Americans and they chose the most public occasions for their demonstrations for the cause. Roberta Gibb did it first at Boston in 1966. The organisers did not recognise her presence, she was not given a number and did not submit to the obligatory physical examination before the race. But she ran the distance, and by knowing which man she finished with knew her official time was 3hrs 21min 40sec.

A year later she ran again, again unofficially and this time more slowly. But without a start number officials still regarded the masculine purity of their race as unsullied.

But that same year, 1967, another women, Katherine Switzer finally cracked the system. It was all rather simple. She entered simply as K. Switzer. Nobody asked her sex, and she did not mention it. She was given the registration number 261, skipped the medical but turned up to run.

Her appearance would not have attracted any more media attention that year than Roberta Gibb's but for one over-zealous Boston official, John Semple. He spotted her from the accompanying bus, leapt off and attempted to push her out of the race. He failed. Switzer was running with her large boyfriend, Thomas Miller, who dispatched Semple with some ease. A photographer

happened to record the scenes, and women's marathon running gained more world-wide attention than ever.

'I'm not against women athletes,' said Semple later. 'But international rules bar men and women from the same race and our rules limit this race to men'.

The writing though was on the wall, or at least the road. Boston attracted more women the following two years while still refusing to accord them official status. But the cracks were showing. America's Road Runners Club staged its first official championship for women in 1970. Boston finally conceded two years later but integration was not total. The numbers issued to the nine women runners were all prefixed with the letter F.

A mother of three won that Boston women's race but far more slowly than in other races. The previous year a 19-year-old American Elizabeth Bonner ran a world fastest, and an Australian woman finally shattered the three hour barrier in one enormous leap by 13½ minutes. Within weeks several women had followed.

The 2:40 barrier succumbed in 1975 and in 1979 Norwegian teacher Greta Waitz, an international class track runner who had frequently won the women's world cross country championship, swept through 2:30 in New York. A year later she lowered it again to below 2:26, a time which would have won her the Olympic silver medal as recently as 1956. Women were fast catching up.

The women's cause achieved an unwelcome promotion in 1980 when a 26-year-old Cuban-born New Yorker Rosie Ruiz was struck off the finishing lists of both New York and Boston marathons after claims that she had cheated.

The claims were made by her rivals after she had crossed the line first in a stunning 2:31:56, the third fastest time by a woman. For one thing she did not appear to be tired, and for another her thighs were clearly too well-endowed for a runner. When reporters questioned her about her 'splits', she was nonplussed. 'That girl's a phoney,' said top runner Patti Lyons.

Soon it became apparent that Rosie had joined the race in the last mile or two. Nobody had seen her before that. Then, on checking her only previous marathon 'time' in New York, where she had been credited with 2:56, it was discovered she had been seen travelling on the subway towards the Central Park finish during the race! The New York organisers amended her performance to read 'non-finisher' and Boston disqualified her. But, if this cloud had a silver lining, it was the enormous publicity generated for women marathoners.

Women, of course, remain a tiny majority but only because the numbers of men running have grown so vastly. In the first London marathon in 1980, there were 300 women, three times the usual total entry for races a few years earlier. There just happened to be 20 times as many men that day!

But the important fact was that they had made their point. Women could survive a marathon, and do well at it. The International Amateur Athletic Federation finally agreed, America and then Britain in 1975 made their participation permissible and in 1982 women will make their marathon debut in a major championship, the European in Athens. Two years later, the IOC have agreed to make them welcome, too, in the Los Angeles Olympics.

But so much of this boom in running, and particularly in marathon running, was in America. What was happening elsewhere? In marathons, it must be said, there was little activity. What had been exported successfully were 'fun runs', a non-competitive gathering of joggers who rarely ran more than two or three miles. Whole families participated, and the only prize was generally a certificate to confirm completion of the course. In one in London in 1979, sponsored by the *Sunday Times*, 15,000 were persuaded to jog round a 2½ mile grassy course in Hyde Park. A similar venture in New Zealand drew 30,000 and one in Italy 55,000!

These were the seeds of the marathon boom. People were running. They needed a goal, something more substantial and exciting than a 'fun run'. It had to be the marathon. But how could they enter? Established British marathons demanded a qualifying time for entry, or at least a good class 20 mile race time. Many of those wanting to try were not even members of clubs, another requirement.

The New York City race had no such restrictions and no qualifying time. It welcomed everybody. The only restriction on the field was the number of runners the organisers and the police could handle. It was first-come, first-served, and foreigners were even offered special facilities and quotas. In 1979, 100 Britons and an even greater number of French crossed the Atlantic to try it.

One was Chris Brasher, Olympic steeplechase champion of 1956 and then a balding but active journalist of 50. He ran, and then wrote about it in *The Observer*.

'To believe this story,' he began, 'you must believe that the human race can be one joyous family, working together, laughing together, achieving the impossible.

'I believe it because I saw it happen. Last Sunday, in one of the most violent, trouble-stricken cities in the world, 11,532 men, women and children from 40 countries of the world, assisted by

2.5 million black, white and yellow people, Protestants and Catholics, Jews and Muslims, Buddhists and Confucians, laughed, cheered and suffered during the greatest folk festival the world has seen.'

It was emotive stuff, and he concluded with a challenge to his own country's capital city: 'I wonder whether London could stage such a festival? We have the course, a magnificent course. But do we have the heart and hospitality to welcome the world?'

For months he waited for the response. It never came. So Brasher took matters into his own hands. He recruited like-minded enthusiasts, flew back to America to seek their advice, and hawked his dream around boardrooms of London. The Greater London Council gave its blessing and support, the police agreed it would make a change from handling demonstrators and soccer hooligans and the Gillette company pledged the first £50,000 needed to get it off the ground. In October, 1980, the first London marathon was announced for the following March.

Brasher anticipated that the record British field of around 700 would be exceeded. He thought, perhaps, that 4,000 might want entries and some of those would drop out on the day. He did not expect to be swamped by 21,000 requests. When he was it signalled not just the arrival of marathon madness in Britain but a mania for it in the media.

There were Members of Parliament, 70-year-olds, a zoo owner, a blind man who needed to be roped to his companion. There was a waiter who intended running in full uniform balancing a tray with a glass and bottle on it. There was the disc jockey, Jimmy Savile, who was intending to run in a gold lamé track suit. There were numerous grandfathers and grandmothers, an international rugby player, a Fleet Street gossip columnist and even a few international runners. Everyone had a story to tell, and the papers for months were full of them.

In 1981 it was an event rivalled in London only by the Royal Wedding. Television devoted the bulk of its outside broadcast team to cover it. And for weeks before it the parks and streets of the capital were paved with runners.

Runners were no longer an oddity to be scorned and ridiculed. The media made them the heroes of their time. For the first time they could run with their heads high through busy streets in daylight. The City was bouncing with them at lunchtimes.

The day itself, March 29, was perfect. It was cool and damp. More than 7,000 of those who had been granted the coveted entries turned up, massed under the brooding grey skies of Greenwich Park in South East London, a sea of humanity which packed the road gutter to gutter for half a mile. At 9am precisely a naval canon fired.

The leaders were off; the others hardly moved. For almost six minutes those at the back of the press waited patiently to make the first stride. Some took 6½ minutes to even cross the starting line.

Thousands had turned out to cheer them. 'Like a football crowd,' said one report. Those who gave up, beaten they thought by their own frailty, were shouted and cheered back into action. 'You can do it, mate' came the cries. 'Stick with it'.

Incredibly, the vast majority made it. Through Woolwich, round the famous *Cutty Sark*, over Tower Bridge, through the Isle of Dogs and Dockland, past the Tower of London and along the Embankment and under Big Ben and into Constitution Hill for the finish. The course, remeasured later, proved to be 30 metres too long but nobody was beaten by that much at the end.

Indeed, fewer than ten percent were defeated by the complete distance. Of the 7,055 official starters, 6,418 finished, 1,294 of them beating three hours. At the front there was a dead heat for first between the American Dick Beardsley and the Norwegian Inge Simonsen in 2:11:48, the fastest time recorded in an English marathon.

More significantly, 406 runners finished inside 2:40, far more than had done so in New York from its numerically greater field.

The MPs finished, the DJ finished, the race's own doctor finished and the gossip columnist finished. Race director Chris Brasher finished inside three hours which was fine for a man of 52, and a mother of two, Joyce Smith, became the third women ever to run inside 2:30. Trevor Wright, of Wolverhampton, finished third in the race, and stayed at the finish to see his wife Rosemary finish inside three hours. And 78-year-old Bob Wiseman was still running when most had gone home, and he finished too in 6¼ hours.

Leslie Watson finished, and at the age of 33 that was her 48th marathon. 'Today was fabulous,' she said. 'Next best to New York, and that's unbelievable but this is close. But then they've had loads of marathons and it's our first'.

Madge Sharples, a 64-year-old diplomat's wife, finished after adjourning to a St John's Ambulance post after 10 miles where a strong cup of tea cured her, she said, of buttock cramp.

At the finish every one was wrapped in a silver foil space blanket and, as one reporter put it, 'wandered off up Piccadilly looking like oven-ready chickens'. More than 1,000 volunteers from athletics clubs, rugby clubs and local authorities had handed out 2,000 blankets, 400 gallons of coffee, 5,000 apples and 50,000 plastic cups en route. There were also 5,000 special constables on duty, 300 St John's ambulancemen and 75 portable loos.

Fred Lebow, the director who had turned an ordinary park race into the New York classic in a decade, ran the London with the number 0001, and was impressed. 'In many respects it surpassed New York,' he said. 'It took us a decade to get the kind of crowd out that London had. I think Londoners should be very proud.'

'Catch on?' asked the *Daily Mail* rhetorically the next morning. 'Nobody will be able to stop it now. This show will run and run.'

Four hours running had brought a capital city to a standstill, and its citizens delighted in it. Co-winner Dick Beardsley said it for everybody: 'What does it matter who wins anyway. As far as I'm concerned anyone who finishes this thing is a winner.' And London, too, knew they had a winner.

Brasher predicted that in 1982 there would be thousands more disappointed because they could not be accomodated. 'Police say they could handle 20,000 but we organisers can't,' he said. 'We'll put a limit of 14,000 for '82 but I'll have 40 or 50,000 entry forms printed just in case.'

His foresight was too cautious. When entries opened again, the recreation department of Greater London Council was overwhelmed with nearly 90,000 applications. One came from East Ender Paul Summers, the only real casualty of the first race. He had run 20 miles with a stress fracture and ended with a complete fracture. He was in hospital for several weeks but was determined to be fit to complete the course at the second attempt. Another came from a woman already seven months pregnant. 'Is four months after giving birth long enough to train, she asked Brasher.

The response was as great in the rest of the country. Other cities sought to emulate London. A Peoples Marathon in Solihull had more than 1,900 finishers. The established Sandbach marathon for more serious racers attracted 600 for the first time, the Great North Run, a half-marathon on Tyneside, around 12,500 and the largest of all full marathons in 1981 was a Manchester race with 8,753 runners and, by police estimates, a million spectators.

For 1982, Wolverhampton announced it would host a marathon, and so did Sheffield. Manchester planned another, and Birmingham their own. The Road Runners Club estimated that by the end of 1981 there had been 40, and expected 50 the following year. So enormous was the demand that the Amateur Athletic Association set up a special committee under its own president, former marathoner Squire Yarrow, to coordinate dates.

Nor was the enthusiasm confined to Britain. There were 1,500 finishers in an Oslo race and 6,500 in Stockholm. When the New York marathon came round in October, director Fred Lebow confessed that he could have filled all 16,000 places with foreigners so great was the demand. As it was there were 700 Britons and almost as many French, and all told 40 countries represented.

In Britain, London's race made two more significant changes. Pressure on the AAA forced them to reduce their minimum permitted age two years to 18, and within months the women followed suit, bringing their minimum down from 21. First to benefit was 20-year-old Kate FitzGibbin who won a Manchester charity marathon three weeks after the rule change and with it a free trip to the next Boston.

Prizes of that value are a new phenomenon. Large fields mean large kitties — the 1982 London race have charged between £4 and £8 to enter and prizes have become so generous that they threaten a runner's amateur status. The trip to Boston is acceptable only because it can be put down as legitimate travelling expenses to a competition but in fact it far exceeds the permitted 250 dollars.

The marathon's popularity in the Eighties is having the same effect as did its previous boom after Dorando's race — professionalism. Where there is a market there is soon a trader wanting to profit by it. In America already there is a fully-fledged professional circuit, and the danger is that the entire sport of road running could be damaged.

Road runners rightly feel that if promoters and major companies are willing to offer them large cash prizes as a reward for their talent, there is no good reason not to accept. The International Amateur Athletic Federation might ban them from future amateur competition but that is small beer to runners whose ambitions probably never included an Olympics. Only track runners are deterred from open professionalism by such threats.

So the creation of several rival governing bodies claiming to represent runners in America happened in 1980. The Athletic Congress, America's national government for athletics, was the harassed parent, unable to keep control of rebellious adolescents.

The Association of Track and Field Athletes (ATFA) was formed largely representing athletes who perform within a stadium. The Association of Road Racing Athletes (ARRA) comprised the top Americans such as Herb Lindsay, Bill Rodgers, Frank Shorter and Don Kardong. Just to add to the confusion the race directors formed their own Long Distance Race Directors Association (LDRDA), representing the directors of such classic marathons as New York, Boston and the women's Avon.

At first it looked possible that they could work together within the amateur structure. The TAC reached an agreement with the ARRA for a Grand Prix of races in which those who ran for prize money could compete in the same race as amateurs, the only stipulation being that the cash went directly to the runners' clubs.

But the first major sponsors, clothing manufacturer Jordache, did not like the compromise, went ahead with an openly professional race in Atlantic City, and Ron Nabers and women's winner Doreen Ennis both collected 15,000 dollars and a life ban from amateur races. Finally the ARRA met and threw out TAC's Grand Prix scheme.

The TAC has little to offer road runners. Amateur status is of little value to them since the marathon is the only road race on the Olympic programme, and even that was taken away in 1980 by their own Government's boycott of the Moscow Games.

Finally in 1981 the ARRA put together its own run-for-pay circuit. The first race was on June 28, at the existing Cascade Run Off in Portland, Oregon. It was the first of a circuit including six races in 1981 and 15 in 1982 offering prize money of at least 30,000 dollars per race and a 200,000 dollars championship race at the end of the 1982 campaign.

The first race was only 15 kilometres, and the winner Greg Meyer collected 10,000 dollars. Immediately TAC threatened all those who had run with a ban, since running against a professional is a *crime* for an amateur under IAAF rules. The TAC summoned 13 known competitors to a disciplinary hearing in Chicago. Meyer, Rodgers and Lindsay among them.

Only Lindsay bothered to attend, and the cases of all were postponed. Meanwhile the New Zealand Athletic Federation acted more swiftly to ban three of its women who took money in Portland. A few weeks later the first professional marathon was run at Eugene, Oregon, and one of those banned Kiwis, Lorraine Moller, picked up another cheque, this time for 20,000 dollars.

The threat to the amateur sport lies in the rule which costs an amateur his status merely by association in a race with a professional. The 'contamination rule' is what Americans call it. Several top British runners, like Mike McLeod, unwilling to lose their right to run for Britain, had to forego the pleasure of running in the Eugene marathon, a trip McLeod had earned as his prize for winning the Tyneside half-marathon. The sport is being split by it, forcing professionals into their own world again.

That will be a tragedy. The strength of the new 'citizen marathoner' breed is that all run for running's sake. Cash is not their motivation; yet neither are they aiming for the Olympics, to run for Britain or even in most cases to become a member of a club. If somebody offered them a cash prize for finishing a marathon, most would take it without any moral dilemma. Most would not even be aware of any distinction existing between runners.

Don Kardong, the ARRA's president, said: 'It became apparent to us that we would have to organise our own circuit in order to meet our goals of bringing about open competition, enabling athletes to control their own competitive careers and creating a sound foundation for the future of road running. This circuit marks an end to the hypocritical system of "shamateurism" which has prevailed for years.'

Road running and marathoning have little to do with track and field, and do not suffer from athletic's promotional problem of diversity. Track and field is running, jumping, throwing and hurdling done over a multitude of distances and in different ways with little obvious connection. The marathon, like tennis and golf, is a single identifiable event easily promoted and attractive to market. It would lose next to nothing by the loss of its Olympic status, and is most likely to be the branch of the sport which first opens its competition to paid and unpaid together.

Already another American organisation, the 100,000 membership Road Runners Club of America (RRCA) is advising its 400 branches to allow all runners to compete together, regardless of whether they have accepted prize money. Its president Jerry Kokesh says: 'It's pure hypocrisy to ban those who take prize money openly while allowing those who take money under the table to compete.'

Typical of that attitude was the final TAC decision to ban eight of the prize winners in the Portland race while taking no action against Bill Rodgers who has openly admitted to an annual income running into hundreds of thousands of dollars from his athletic and related activities but declined to take the prize money offered to him openly at Portland. Nobody was blaming Rodgers, only the dual-standards of the amateur system.

Of course, the citizen marathoners about to take to the roads for the first time will not need to concern themselves with the problem of accepting prize money. Their only concern will be finishing. But it is as well to be aware that some races are fraught with problems.

You could be 'contaminated' by that affliction called professionalism. One woman who had never bettered four hours entered herself for the professional section of the Eugene marathon inadvertently. She did not win a prize but she may have lost her right to run in future amateur races by mischance.

Some marathons do not welcome the inexperienced runner. They set standards to keep them out, either demanding a previous quality performance in a marathon or a 20 mile time. Others are open only to members of a club affiliated to a national governing body, such as the Amateur Athletic Association in England or its equivalent elsewhere.

Some, of course, welcome only the citizen marathoner. They may disqualify the better runners. The People's Marathon in Chelmsley Wood, near Birmingham, will not accept runners who have finished faster than 2:28 in the last year or so.

Others such as London and New York are happy to mix the types, welcoming as many first timers and 10 minute mile pace runners as regulars and stars. New York had 4,000 first timers in 1981. Races like their's have the facilities and the vast armies of volunteers, that enable them to keep a course in operation long after the average marathon. Arrive four hours after the start at some British races and you will not find officials there to welcome you. They will have gone home!

New York is the classic now among the twin-role races since Boston set standards to keep numbers within manageable bounds. For four successive years now, the women's world best has fallen there, and Alberto Salazar's world best in 1981 set the final seal of approval.

Salazar, of course , made his marathon debut in the New York race in 1980, and won it. Indeed, it was not just his first marathon but his first run beyond eight miles. And he became the second fastest American ever and the seventh fastest anywhere at the first attempt. At the second attempt a year later he became the world record holder.

But then Salazar was a fine runner of repute before he tried a marathon. He still regards himself as a 10,000 metres track runner. Others in the New York race making their debuts have far different backgrounds.

Joe Michael's dream of running the race in 1981 began when he fired his doctors who told him to take it easy after his seventh coronary had forced him to have major heart surgery. Michael's first attack came at the age of 27. 'I was overweight, eating junk food, smoking four packs of cigarettes a day and doing a lot of drugs,' he recalls.

'Actually, I consider the heart attacks were blessings because they led to a change in lifestyle. Like an idiot, though, it took seven of them to wake me up to the fact that I couldn't even lift my eight year old son.

'Then it dawned on me that I wasn't going to die of a heart attack but of a broken heart hanging around my home. So I got rid of those sedentary doctors who told me all the time to take it easy and entered a rehabilitation programme.'

Ruth Rothfarb, who reckons she gave up having to take drugs for her arthritis once she started running, also ran. She is 80. It wasn't her first. She completed the Ottawa Marathon two months earlier in 70F/21C heat.

So did Noel Johnson. He started running when he was 70 and 40 pounds heavier. 'I'd boxed as a youth but for 40 years I'd smoked at least 30 cigarettes a day and cigars and pipes,' he says. He also developed a heart condition. He ran his first marathon at 72 in 4:45, and has now run the New York three times. This year when he did it he was 82! 'I'll keep coming back,' he said. 'I plan to write a book on it in 2000AD.'

The stories of those who have been inspired to try and have succeeded in New York are endless. Dick Traum tried it on an artificial leg and John Kelley tried it for the 51st time. Mort Schlein ran it although he is blind and an English chef Dale Lyons ran it carrying a pancake.

Of course, these are only the more unusual which the organisers broadcast for the benefit of the media which masses for the race. Every runner has a story of his own. So does the race itself.

It could be the story of the 68,000 safety pins kept along the route in case of elastic failure in runners' shorts. Or the 100 foot (30 metre) urinal at the start line on Staten Island which organisers boast is the world's largest. Or the 284 gallons of paint it took to mark a blue line for 26.2 miles. Or the 20,920 gallons of water drunk or splashed on. Not to mention the 1,200 doctors and nurses on call.

In the end, of course, the marathon is only ever about those who run it. They will have come in all shapes and sizes. Scientists say those who carry only 2lb for every inch of height are best suited physically. Salazar, at 6ft and 143lb, meets the qualification precisely. So does the 5ft 7in Waldemar Cierpinski, and he is Olympic champion.

But 10 women and 1,507 men at the 1981 New York race ordered commemorative T-shirts in an 'extra large' size, and they certainly could not have been of optimum scientific size. One was former world heavyweight champion Ingemar Johansson, who ran both Stockholm and New York marathons and weighed in at 240lb.

That's the great thing about marathons. It takes all sorts.

CHAPTER 3

How to Start

RUNNING is the classically simple, democratic sport. The popular slogan of the Seventies was 'Sport For All' and that is precisely what running is. To start, you need very little in the way of expensive equipment; you don't need partners, an opponent or a team; you don't even need skill. For taking up jogging as a first step to marathon running — and it's not such a massive step as thousands of ordinary people in Britain and America have shown in recent years — depends on just one person: YOU.

Here you are in a comfortable armchair. Not far away is your front door. Just beyond is the street and the beginning of a new hobby for some, an entirely new way of life for others. It all depends on what you want to get out of your running. Approach it in the right way and you will get fun, increased well-being, a trimmer shape, a brighter complexion. But experts and novices alike agree that all those benefits, pleasant as they are, pale against the entirely intangible result of finishing a marathon. You have probably met someone experiencing post-marathon euphoria a few days after the race. They're the ones who can't walk without a grimace but who are nevertheless wrapped in a great, encompassing smile. It's the smile of an achiever, someone who has dared and succeeded. That achievement makes you feel different inside, makes you think differently and more positively about yourself. If anyone has ever told you that you are no good at something, this is your private answer back.

In recent years only one thing has saddened me as a participant in the marathon boom. That is the reaction of some of the country's more experienced runners, the lifelong athletes who are the backbone of the British athletics club system, the most extensive and successful in the world. There is a feeling among some of them that their cosy little world should be protected from outsiders with no background in the sport and one or two clubs and race organisers have effectively said to newcomers: 'Keep out — real athletes only'.

But what is a 'real' athlete? Is it the club runner who's taken his best years to reach a 2:50 marathon or the gifted newcomer who, after a decade and more of inactivity or sporadic football matches, reaches the same standard at his first or second attempt? And what about the mother of three who in her 30s uses some of her new-found freedom from the kids to do a bit of training for the first time since school Sports Day and finds running a sub-three hour marathon rather easier than a day's housework?

Suddenly, the special privileges which come from the membership of a small, closed community such as an old-fashioned athletics club don't seem to count for so much. 'I run marathons' is no longer the badge of loftiness and loneliness and no longer the signal for bemused looks from outsiders. The marathon runner, in other words, is no longer quite so special. The marathon runner is just Everyman and that fact diminishes the stature of some who sought to be different through running.

That is not an ignoble quest: asked a few years ago why I ran, I responded that as well as enjoying it for itself, it was what I did. 'It's what makes me different,' I said. I couldn't make the same response nowadays with quite the same assurance, but I'm pretty certain I could find some new reasons if I really needed to!

So, while there's plenty of magic about the marathon event, as Chapters One and Two have shown, there's no special mystique about the people who run marathons, no special qualifying or disqualifying factors once you have made up your mind that this is what you want to do. And your mind is perhaps more important than you realise at this stage.

For while you can't get out of your chair and into the street just by thinking and dreaming about it, you just as surely won't keep your feet pointing in the right direction for long unless your mind makes a positive decision — an act of will — to commit yourself to the long, often hard but ultimately rewarding road.

All runners, new or old, fast or slow, have the same decision to make again and again: the decision to get changed and get out there on the road, even though there may be more inviting things to do.

I used to think that star runners don't have the same fleshly weaknesses as ordinary mortals, the same nagging voice in the mind which says, 'Let's have a rest today, it won't matter, nobody will know'. But virtually every top marathoner I have ever spoken to has confirmed that the toughest step is always the first one – the one which takes them to the front door and beyond.

Before You Run

The decision and commitment, therefore, is all down to you. But before you make that important step towards the door should you take advice from anyone else? And what about a medical check-up?

First, the medical aspect. The usual safety-first advice is to get the medical go-ahead if you have any lingering doubts about your health, or if you are over 35 and have not exercised in any regular fashion for 10 years or more, or if you suffer from a weight or blood pressure problem at any age. Or try this test: walk very briskly for five minutes. If 10 minutes after stopping you are still breathless or your pulse is still over 100 beats per minute, consult your doctor.

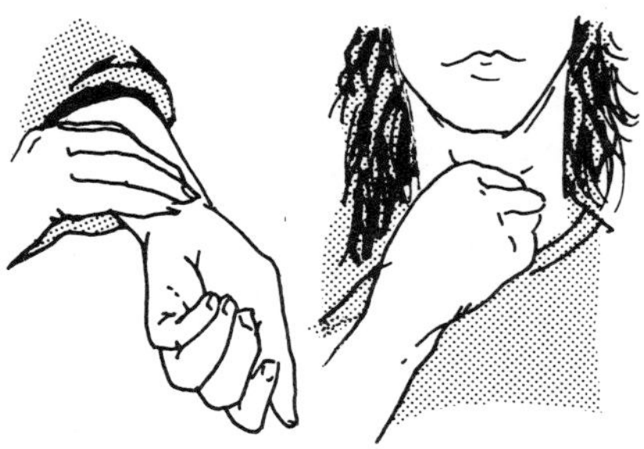

Two ways of taking your pulse.

You would be surprised at the therapeutic benefits jogging can bring. The General Council and Register of Osteopaths in the UK has come down firmly in favour of gentle jogging for those with certain types of routine back trouble and there are asthmatics, diabetics and sufferers from diseases such as cystic fibrosis who jog, run and race successfully.

Their secret is that they took advice and started very gently and sensibly; indeed, many people with a pre-existing medical condition have been advised to take up exercise by their doctors as more members of the medical profession have come to appreciate the value of the cardio-vascular (heart and lung) health promoted by jogging and running.

That said, however, it is rather more difficult to answer the question 'where do I go for a check-up, should I want one?' Many GPs simply do not have the time, and sometimes the interest, to start giving preventive check-ups, unless someone like your employer or insurance company is paying. In addition, the value of 'static' check-ups may be called into question. An exercise stress test would reveal much more about your fitness, but the UK, unlike the USA, does not have a network of such facilities which means that you may have a search on your hands. Ask your doctor first; then try one of the private medical chains.

Common sense will generally tell you whether it's safe to start and the statistics are very much on your side, provided you follow the simple guidelines we give below.

Then there is the question of advice and company. You can get all the advice you'll need initially within this book and from those listed in Chapter 9. Company is a matter of personal choice. It's not a sacred right of the long (or even short) distance runner to be lonely and perhaps the biggest single reason for the recent growth of the sport is its sociability. People have fun running together and get a kick out of supporting each other and helping each other keep going. If you know that someone else is going to be there waiting to go out with you, you are less likely to take the easy way out and skip it 'just this once'.

Husband and wife partnerships are a natural, often successful combination. Bob and Sammy Green in Buckinghamshire are good examples. One Christmas, they each bought the other a track suit as an incentive to get fit. On New Year's Day, hungover and tired, they kept their promises to each other and went out for a painful, panting jog. During their first few runs, various neighbours saw them and asked could they join in, too.

They decided to make the group more formal with set meeting times and the result was the foundation of Burnham Joggers, perhaps Britain's best known and most successful jogging group. Bob is a local doctor who prescribes exercise before pills where possible and his wife Sammy is a three-hour marathoner who still insists the Burnham group's main role is that of mutual encouragement.

Another virtue of joining a club or informal group is the repository of local and expert information you will find there. Another famous jogging club is Birmingham's Centurion Joggers, promoters of the annual, original People's Marathon. They made contact early on with a local college's physiology department and arranged their own medicals. Says their founder John Walker: 'The reason so many of our people stick with it rather than falling by the wayside are the tangible signs of progress.' The regular tests show them decreases in weight, body fat and heart rate and increases in oxygen uptake and other indicators of cardio-vascular efficiency.

A formal club may not be the right format for you. If you're not an out-and-out loner (and many people do prefer to enjoy their training runs as a precious bit of time to themselves) a friend, relative or neighbour might make the task a bit easier and more enjoyable. If you would like to sample the atmosphere in a club — athletics or jogging — Chapter 9 will tell you how to go about finding one in your area.

Running Shoes

Running is not an equipment-intensive sport, but the equipment it does involve is vitally important. If you want to do everything 'properly' from the start, purchasing every item of customised clothing and every bit of gadgetry to go with it, you could say goodbye to £250, maybe more. That's up to you; all that is really necessary is a tenth of that figure in the first place. And for equipment, read shoes.

Consider these facts: in a mile of jogging the average 10½ stone man strikes the ground 800 times with each foot. That's a cumulative force of 60 tons per foot per mile, which means you need firm cushioning to protect your feet and the rest of your body from the damaging shockwaves. The only time this rule does not apply is if you live on an isolated beach spoiled by neither man-made debris nor rocks and pebbles. Then your equipment cost is zero as you will be running happily barefoot, the way you were designed to do in the first place. In such idyllic circumstances, it is unlikely that you will need this book to tell you about the joys of running but the vast majority have to run on the unfriendly and unnatural surface of tarmac and pavement.

Hence the importance of a pair of proper, specialised running shoes, bought from a specialist running store. Plimsolls and the cheap 'trainers' you can buy in bins from ordinary shoe shops should be avoided as a false economy. Padded tennis shoes are better, but they are not designed for pounding around on tarmac.

There is not a single 'best buy' in the running shoe jungle (the best running shops stock over 100 models from perhaps 20 manufacturers from all over the world) for the simple reason that no two pairs of feet are alike. There is the shape of your foot to consider (fit) the speed and frequency of your running (the build of the shoe) and the terrain you intend to run on (the sole/grip).

As a beginner, you should ask to be directed to the road training shoe category. Lightweight racing shoes will come later (they could be positively harmful at this stage of your career) as will specialised soles for country training (even the country dweller will spend much of his/her time on the roads).

Here is a checklist of the things to look for when buying your first pair of shoes, along with a diagram of a typical shoe showing the areas to which you should give special attention and explaining some of the 'technospeak' the shoe companies have invented over the years.

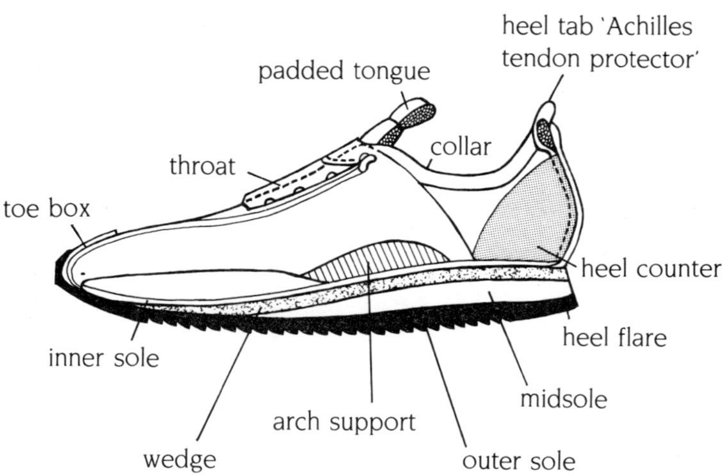

When selecting your running shoes:

● Go to a specialist running shop and check you're being served by someone who knows what they're talking about (i.e. they should be a runner and not afraid to tell you what shoes they wear and why!).

● Wear the socks you will be running in to try on the shoes.

● Walk and jog in the shop in a number of shoes to get the feel of them 'in action' (some shops let you go for a run outside in a 'demo' model — that means they care and deserve your patronage).

● Buy late in the afternoon if possible when your feet are slightly swollen from the day's activities.

● Be prepared to shop around; there are bargains to be had even among the top-rated shoes in specialist shops.

In the shoe itself, look for:

● A snug but not over-tight fit. Allow ½ inch between your big toe and the toe box and make sure you can pinch a small amount of material between your fingers around the toe box area when the shoe is laced securely.

● A smooth inner area with no rough stitching or seams.

● Good cushioning at the heel; if there is a wedge between the midsole and the outer sole, this will usually be pliable to the touch.

● A gently curved heel can be useful to facilitate footplant but the heel flare should not be excessive as this can lead to instability.

● Adequate cushioning at the forefoot: the wedge and/or midsole should not taper so severely as to leave the forefoot unprotected. It is a bad sign if the front of the shoe rises excessively off the floor when placed there empty.

● A padded arch support, soft inner sock and padded tongue.

● Flexibility at the ball of the foot; you should be able to bend an empty shoe at the ball (approximately one third of the shoe's length from the front) with gentle hand pressure.

● A firm and stable heel counter which is not mushy or mobile.

● A padded heel tab above the heel counter (the 'Achilles tendon protector') which is not too high or stiff. This can damage the achilles if permanently rubbing against it.

● A sole that is wide enough to take the whole foot without any overhang (i.e. the upper should not be bulging over the edge of the inner sole which is sometimes much less broad than the outer sole).

Other Kit

After shoes, clothing is the next essential. My advice, initially, is to spend nothing: just look in your wardrobe and adapt. Few people have the confidence to appear in public immediately in shorts and vest (and in all but the best summer weather in Britain, that is not really advisable anyway) but most have a track suit from some sports-playing period in their lives. If you don't have a track suit, use an old sweat shirt or sweater and a pair of loose slacks. Underneath, a T-shirt and underpants/pants are all that is required in normal weather conditions.

But such gear is just for the acclimatising period when you're deciding that running is, after all, for you and when you're also trying your best not to look too conspicuous (that sweater will hide the pot belly better than a sleek, contoured track suit, for example).

Soon, though, you'll want to look the part in functional, smart clothing suited to running. Quite apart from the definite psychological lift of feeling good because you look good, you will be more comfortable.

Track Suits

Unlike shoes, it's not essential to buy these from the specialist stores. Things to look for: a tapered leg (not straight or, even more ridiculous flared: they are for the sporty types you only ever see propping up bars) preferably with zips at the bottom to facilitate removal over shoes and stirrups to prevent riding up the legs. Pockets with zips in either the jacket or the trousers are useful. Check the jacket, if zipped, is not too tapered to the waist: if there is too much elastication at the waist, the jacket tends to ride up, leading to an exposed and cold midriff. Prices range from £10-£40, depending on material, style and prevailing fashion.

An alternative to a straight track suit is to buy a sweat top (hooded tops are excellent for winter training) and separate pants (often called tracksters) which can be lighter than conventional track suit trousers.

Shirts

T-shirts are ideal in summer but you'll probably appreciate a soccer or rugby shirt in colder weather. Make sure your shirts are not too tight at the neck and under the armpits.

Shorts

You may be able to manage with soccer or rugby shorts, but these can be a bit constricting for running. Best to get a proper pair; I prefer cotton or one of the modern cotton/nylon mixtures in preference to pure nylon which tends to rub more when in contact with skin, especially inside the thighs. Always try shorts on in the shop to see how they move when you raise one leg so that the thigh is parallel to the floor. For men, the 'freedom short' with gusset is popular and there is a unisex style of more square-cut shorts which many women road runners now wear in preference to the traditional athletic briefs which may make the beginner a little too self-conscious. Try to find shorts with a seamless seat, and study the seams elsewhere in the shorts to make sure the stitching is not rough.

Underneath

Cotton pants — more absorbent than other man-made materials — are recommended for ladies. In winter or cooler summer evenings, many lady runners wear tights too, either instead of or in addition to track suit bottoms. Most men steer clear of conventional athletic supports or jock straps as they can become cumbersome and stiff with frequent wear and washing. They are also less warm in winter (do not laugh: learned papers have been written on frost-bite of a runner's Vital Parts in American medical journals!). Again, cotton, one-piece briefs are best but do check that they are not too tightly elasticated at the crotch and that the crotch is reasonably wide. Otherwise you can end up with an uncomfortable single strand of material slowly strangling you between the legs. Remember, running is going to teach you a lot about parts of your body — and the way they work — that you never dreamed of before!

An extra consideration for the ladies is whether to wear a bra. Unless you never find it necessary to wear a bra, you will almost certainly want to have the support of one when running. Try jogging on the spot indoors to see how much of a nuisance 'bounce' might be. If you feel at all uncomfortable or self-conscious, experiment with your regular bras to see which suits you best for running.

Many women have found conventional 'fashion' bras to be unsuitable for running: the straps slip, it rides up and the metal and plastic bits chafe. As a result, there are now several sports bras on the market (look for the Warner, Berlei, Triumph and Gossard brands). These tend to be one-piece, elasticated, and made in 'breathable' material. They should prevent chafing and embarrassment.

Socks

Again, cotton or wool are best for the absorbency. You can also buy special running socks with extra cushioning at the major pressure points and a sort of arch support as well. The latter ought not to necessary if you've got the right type of shoe.

Nightwear

One consideration when choosing clothing is that much of your training may have to be done at night in the dark. Light coloured garments are obviously desirable and it is worth buying some fluorescent strips of material for your track suit or even a custom-made orange jacket or bib from running or cycle stores, to ensure visibility and maximum safety.

Extras

A pair of cotton gloves are a must on cold winter's days. Cotton because anything else will be too bulky and it's rare that you will keep your gloves on the whole way once you get moving and build up a sweat. When you take them off, cotton gloves are light enough to tuck in your waist band or stuff in your pocket. A woollen hat can be useful in winter (especially if you suffer from cold ears or earache) and while it's true that a very large proportion of body heat is lost through the head, some people begin to feel over-warm after only a few minutes' running enclosed in a hat.

So there are your clothing needs. As you will see, much of the gear need not be bought specially but if you are going to invest in specialist items, go to a running shop and look over the range and get the advice of running assistants there. The basic rule is, if it feels comfortable, wear it. It's not how you look, it's how you feel that counts.

Other Equipment

Other equipment can generally be classed as luxuries or inessentials. You could buy a blood pressure kit, a pacer (a bleeper that sets a pace like a metronome), a computerised pulse counter (I prefer fingers) or a pouch for keys, ID, money etc which fixes on to your shoe laces.

One everyday item you need on the run is a watch. Not only might you enjoy yourself so much you lose track of time, you will be dealing in minutes rather than miles in the early days of your training. You may also want to check your pulse against a watch. A conventional stopwatch is not necessary for this and is in any case difficult to carry. Obviously, it helps if your wristwatch has a stop-watch function, as many now do.

Finally, there is one piece of your running equipment which will never leave the house although it's almost as important as your shoes. That is your training diary, in which you record your runs, detailing time and/or distance. See Chapter 4 for further details.

You can use an ordinary desk diary but I recommend one set aside for running alone. You'll find there's plenty to say and it can be an important psychological prop to refer back to your progress, to analyse your highs and lows, when those doubts about 'is it all worth it' crop up.

Some people prefer a wall chart to record training, drawing elaborate graphs of performance and certainly a rising trend in mileage and speed can be a great motivator. There are also special Runners Diaries or logs on the market: here we reprint a page from one of the best.

	Date	Course	Distance	Time	Comments
M	29th	1 x Main Road Loop	2	18	9pm Windy + Wet. Felt O.K
T	30th	Rest			Legs still stiff
W	1st	1 x Main Road Loop	2	17	Feeling better – Legs O.K. Pushed last ½ mile
T	2nd	Club Night group run	2½	20	Carried along by group
F	3rd	Rest			No after effects
S	4th	Playing fields	2	18	Lunchtime – felt good on Grass.
S	5th	Forest Run	4?	40	Longest run yet. V. pleased
		Week's Total	12½		

At home you may also need a simple first-aid kit consisting of the usual items plus surgical spirit (for toughening up the skin of the feet if you are prone to blisters) embrocation or liniment (Dr Sloan's, Mentholatum or similar) for easing stiff muscles and elasticated bandages for support when necessary.

Warming Up

So you are kitted up and ready to go. First, remind yourself this is not a race: you are going to enjoy yourself, not prove yourself against others or the clock. Second, find some spare space in your bedroom or lounge for the following warm-up suppling exercises. If you warm up outside, keep full track suit on until you start running.

The warm-up is important as cold muscles are more easily damaged, especially if they are shortened from lack of regular exercise. These five exercises are recommended before each run:

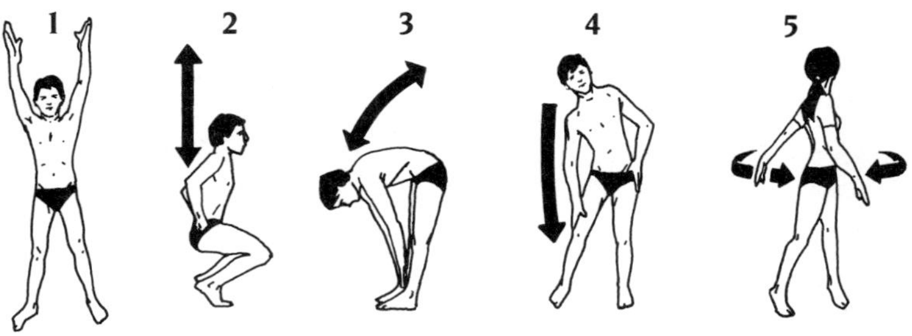

Loosening Exercises

1 Arm movements. With your feet astride, raise your arms. Keeping your body upright, swing both arms forward, then reverse direction. Then swing sideways together, moving your neck and head in the same direction. Then swing your arms in opposite directions to meet at the fingertips behind your neck. Do each movement in each direction about 10 times.

2 Squats. With your hands on hips and keeping a straight back, bend your knees as far as possible, then straighten up to starting position. Aim to reach a position in which your thighs are parallel to the ground, rising on to your toes at the bottom of the movement. Do not use jerky movements, but repeat rhythmically 10 times. Do not do this exercise if you already have trouble with your knees.

3 Forward bend. Again, easy rhythmic movement is required, not stop-start jerks. With your feet together, bend forward to touch your toes with your fingers if you can. Hold temporarily at just short of full extension then ease back upwards. Repeat six times.

4 Side bends. With your feet astride and hands resting on your thighs, lean to the left, looking straight in front of you, and slide your left hand as far down your leg as possible. Hold briefly, then return to start and repeat on the other side, six times on each side.

5 Trunk swinging. With your feet astride, twist to look behind you to the left, then to the right, swinging your arms rhythmically behind you as far as they will go. Do this exercise for 30 seconds.

How Fast, How Far?

If you feel yourself to be very much out of condition when starting to jog for the first time, you may well benefit from a more extended preparatory build-up than that suggested here. If this is the case, the best advice is to refer to the training guidelines offered to beginners in Bruce Tulloh's *The Complete Jogger* (see Chapter 9). That is not to suggest that the beginner's acclimatisation programme offered here is aimed at breaking you in the hard way; simply that it is directed at those who start with a modicum of fitness, perhaps from general games playing.

The first questions beginners usually ask are how fast should I run and then how far? Both are the wrong questions. The early level of effort has nothing to do with speed and we are for the moment concerned with *time* run, rather than distance. Obviously, to achieve a training effect (that is, to teach the body how to take in and process its basic fuel, oxygen) you must put the system under a certain amount of stress, but how much will be determined by how you feel.

There are a number of popular formulae involving pulse rate to regulate the degree of effort in early jogging. A useful one determines the levels you should work within as follows: subtract your age in years from the figure 200 to give your maximum pulse rate in beats per minute (bpm) and subtract your age from 170 for the lower level — below which you are not really working hard enough. Thus a 35-year-old should aim at the 135-165 bpm range.

The only problem with such formulae is that checking your pulse gets in the way of actual running. Apart from the very early runs, when the walking sections can be used, I suggest that if you want your pulse to be your guide you check it only at the start and end of each session, then 10 minutes later to check recovery rate as described above. After all, you have a built-in regulator known as breathlessness.

Use how you feel as a guide to effort in your first runs. If you do get breathless, ease off and walk for a bit if necessary. You shouldn't be panting desperately for air at any stage and if breathlessness becomes dizziness or light-headedness, stop immediately, rest, walk home and seek medical advice before running again.

You will know how you are doing if you use the 'talk test': you should have enough breath left to maintain conversation with a companion while running.

In practice, you will find that even before breathlessness, you may feel limited by tiredness elsewhere (e.g. the calf muscles). Again, be guided by how you feel and don't attempt to push through the pain.

Two principles of training apply equally to the beginner and the hardened marathon runner. The first one is the 'hard-easy' principle whereby the body is allowed to recover after a hard session one day with an easier one the next. In the first few weeks, this should read on-off, allowing one full day's rest between runs. Secondly we have the principle of gradual build-up which is designed to exclude sudden quantum leaps in the amount of stress the body is asked to handle. Even fully trained marathon runners should not increase their weekly training totals by much more than 10 per cent at a time.

Our suggested beginners' programme works on the day-on, day-off principle, taking you through to half an hour's non-stop running in 15 weeks. You may wish to start further into the programme (say week four) or to speed up the process by dropping *some* rest days. But do not skip the days off if you have any ill after-effects from the previous day and do not run more than five times per week.

Beginners' Programme
Figures are minutes of running

	Day						
Week	1	2	3	4	5	6	7
1	5	—	5	—	6	—	6
2	—	7	—	7	—	8	—
3	8	—	9	—	9	—	10
4	—	10	—	11	—	11	—
5	12	—	12	—	13	—	13
6	—	14	—	14	—	15	—
7	15	—	16	—	16	—	17
8	—	17	—	18	—	18	—
9	19	—	19	—	20	—	20
10	—	21	—	21	—	22	—
11	22	—	23	—	23	—	24
12	—	24	—	25	—	25	—
13	26	—	26	—	27	—	27
14	—	28	—	28	—	29	—
15	29	—	30	—	30	—	30

Tips

- Do not go out after a meal until two hours (preferably three) have elapsed.
- There may be days when you feel like doing much more — but resist the temptation until the acclimatisation period is over.
- There will be days when you feel you can't run the whole way. Don't.· Mix jogging with walking, (e.g. alternate minutes of each, or a set number of lamp posts each).
- If you miss a session or sessions through lack of time (or laziness!) go back to the previous session and repeat that before taking up the thread again. If you miss sessions through illness, go back as many sessions as you have missed. (i.e. starting again at a lower level than your last session).
- While the emphasis is on time, an out-and-back route is easiest: if your target is 15 minutes, run 7½ mins out and 7½ mins back.
- If possible, use a mixture of surfaces. Parks and towpaths, apart from aesthetic benefits, offer a chance of escape from jarring on roads.

Style

As with effort, the basic secret is to follow your own inclinations. It is not possible to teach good running style as the adult body will do things that come naturally to it after many years of accommodation. You may not look very pretty, but then the famous Zatopek broke all the so-called rules of good form and still beat the world. Nevertheless, there are certain tips on posture which will make your running life easier.

A lot of tension starts in the upper body, around the neck and in the arms. Don't tense your neck and shoulders and don't grit your teeth. Clenched fists also radiate tension; curl fingers lightly with your thumb resting gently on top of the index finger. Hold your arms easily at your sides, moving in the same direction as you (not high up or across the chest) and keep your eyes aiming about six to eight feet ahead on the road (apart from when dealing with obstacles like cars and people, of course!).

Finally, of greatest importance, don't ape a sprinter's action by landing on your toes. Land as gently as possible on the heel, then 'claw' at the ground as the rest of the foot comes into contact before pivotting off the ball of the foot. It is not necessary to lift the knees high or to take the feet far from the ground.

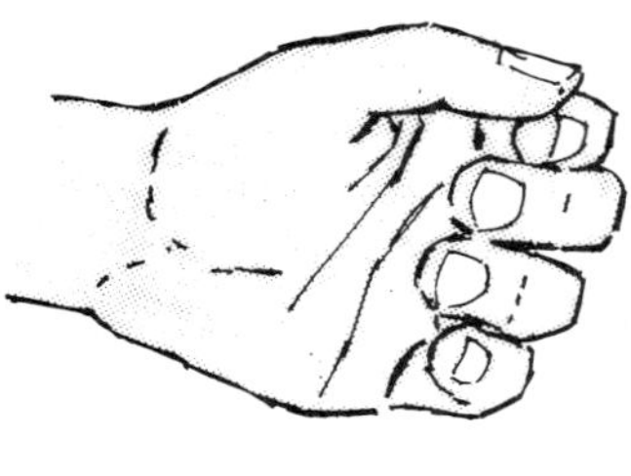

Lightly curled fingers help prevent tension.

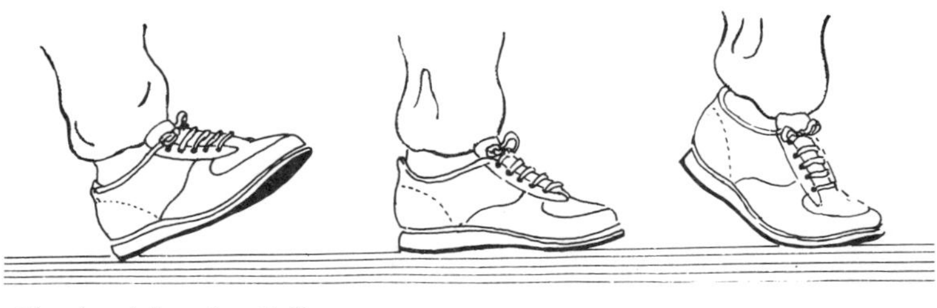

The heel-first footfall.

You will find a natural stride length with training; don't be afraid of starting with little more than a flat-footed shuffle. Once you get going, try to be as erect as possible (check your style in shop windows as you pass!) avoiding the 'sitting-in-a-bucket' posture. This comes from leaning back on your centre of gravity and prevents the supporting leg from straightening correctly when pushing off the ground.

When facing inclines, a slight forward lean from the waist helps as will a degree of shortening of the stride.

Breathing, too, will come naturally. Use nose and mouth fully, breathing as deeply and as rhythmically as possible.

Hazards And Problems

The greatest single hazard the average beginner runner faces is man-made. It is, of course, the tendency to do things too quickly and to ignore the needs and reactions of your body. If you find you are still stiff in the muscles or joints after a day's rest when you come to start your next session, it probably means you overdid the previous run. Don't force yourself on, but take a walk instead and defer the planned session till next time. The schedule here is for advice only: change it and modify it according to your own needs while bearing in mind the principles it is based on.

If you have a bad cold it is inadvisable to run. Certainly, flu-type symptoms and any hint of a fever or raised temperature rule out running completely. To place strain on the heart when it is already coping with a fever can be extremely dangerous.

On the run, perhaps the most constant hazard are loose dogs. Try to spot them in advance and plan your direction accordingly, keeping a wary eye on them. If the brute seems to be interested in you, stop and face it: a sharp reprimand in its direction will usually remove the threat.

Finally, while running can be fun in all kinds of weather, ice poses an obvious problem: if you are on a slippery surface, adopt a more flat-footed posture to maximise grip. The only weather that really rules out running is thick fog: rather than inhaling all the muck, stay indoors and do an extended exercise session.

After The Run

Don't sprint the last few yards, then collapse in a heap. Let your muscles down gently by 'warming down'. Just as important as warming up, this is a way of avoiding lingering muscle stiffness as it keeps the blood circulating fully, counteracting the deposit of 'waste materials' in your muscles. So walk the last couple of hundred yards and/or repeat your starting exercise routine. If you don't shower or bath straight away, put something warm on to stop your sweat cooling you too rapidly.

You may feel like flopping into an armchair, but don't stay there for too long or you may get stiff. Have a bath (which also promotes good circulation) then rest with a refreshing drink.

Women And Running

Apart from the obvious items of clothing, we have made no special reference to the 'problems' of the lady runner. This is because her problems are largely the same as those of the men: she needs will-power, and determination and she's working with the same basic equipment to the same basic end — improving cardiovascular efficiency and the body's response to physical stress.

Many of the old wives' tales you hear are just that. There is no medical basis for the assertion that exercise leads to prolapsed uteruses or damaged breasts. A body that can withstand the rigours of childbirth is not the weak thing many people fondly imagine.

Unless you suffer particularly problematic periods, there is no reason why you should not run at that time of the month (Christa Vahlensieck set the then world record of 2:34:48 in 1977 during her period). Research in the USA shows that painful menstruation is less common among athletes than non-athletes. Further research among top class high mileage women runners showed many had irregular or non-existent periods but as soon as exercise at that level ceased, menstruation returned to normal with no after-effects.

Many women — Margaret Thompson, wife of former Commonwealth and European marathon champion, Ian, is one of them — have continued jogging during pregnancy up to a few weeks before giving birth. It's not advisable to start running for the first time during pregnancy, but if you're already doing so, there's no reason (unless your doctor advises against it) to stop. The rule is to run slowly and comfortably, just ticking over. The time for personal bests and improvement will come later!

The Older Runner

Veteran athletics has, like marathon running, enjoyed a boom period in recent years. People are quite rightly refusing to be put out to grass just because they're no longer at their peak. There are special clubs for veterans (men over 40, women over 35) and most athletics clubs run vets teams. Further details are in Chapter 9.

Here, too, there are no special limitations or qualifications to be made to the advice in this chapter about training and fitness except that as you get older, your muscles lose some of their elasticity and joints are subject to more wear and tear. This means the warm-up exercises are doubly important, as is the advice never to run through stiffness. The heart gradually loses some of its 'pumping power' as you age, but this is reflected in the pulse guidelines given above.

On the positive side, many runners report that the ability to concentrate and endure grows with age, making the going easier in an event like the marathon. Many impetuous youngsters find this is the case when they are passed after 20-odd miles by an ageing body which has been ruled by a head wise in pace judgement!

That there is plenty of potential in non-sporting oldsters is clear. Just think of Jack Foster who started running in his 30s and won the Commonwealth Marathon title in 1974 at age 41, or Madge Sharples who ran her first marathon (the 1981 London) at 64. Just after she turned 65, she knocked over half an hour off her best time in the New York Marathon.

CHAPTER 4

Training

A chain is only as strong as its weakest link. What we have to do is to train all the parts of the body that are stressed in a marathon. The scientific way to train is to identify all the aspects which need improvement and build them up steadily. As training progresses we shall move closer to the racing situation, stressing all the systems at the same time. The different types of training affect different systems, which means that we can have plenty of variety in the early stages of training. It also means that we can do something useful even when some systems have to be rested. This is why some of the training sessions will consist of shorter, faster stretches of running, at a pace much faster than your marathon speed.

Basic principles — overload and recovery

All modern sports training is based on the 'overload' principle. You give the body something to do which is a little more strenuous than it is used to. This puts certain muscles, or perhaps the whole heart-lung system, into a state of stress. The body will then adjust to that stress. If the load is too great, tissues will break down or collapse will follow. This is worse than useless. You may take several days recovering from the damage you have done, and then be back to square one. If the load is too light, the body is not stressed enough and so no adjustment will take place. The art of training lies in finding the right level of stress, and in the last analysis this is up to you.

You will notice that the benefits of training come in the recovery periods between the efforts. It is important that you realise this. Some people think that the more they hurt themselves the more useful the training, but this is just not true. Many dedicated athletes have trained themselves into a state of chronic injury because they did not realise that the rest period is an essential part of the training. The international runner is able to train hard every day because he is fit enough to recover fully in less than 24 hours, but lesser mortals should follow the pattern of alternating hard days and easy days, and in the early stages we shall have a hard day only twice a week.

When you start training, full of enthusiasm, it is very tempting to think that the daily sessions are easy, and you may want to do more. Remember that the training dose should be thought of in terms of weekly and monthly amounts. Too much in the first week may lead to a cutback in the second week.

What we are trying to achieve

The basic necessities of the marathon are obvious — mental determination, physical endurance and enough speed to be able to run faster than 10 minutes per mile, but both endurance and speed depend on other variables. There is 'general endurance', which is a combination of physical and mental toughness often termed 'stamina'. There are dozens of small muscles, tendons and ligaments which are involved in supporting the body's weight during a run, and each one of them has got to be strong enough to maintain normal body posture for the duration of the race. Mental toughness is often greater in the over-30s than in younger people, but unfortunately the sedentary lives which most of us lead bring about weaknesses in these postural muscles, so that you fall into a poor, inefficient running style. General endurance capacity grows rapidly with increasing weekly mileage.

Special endurance, or 'local muscular endurance' refers to the endurance capacity of the major muscle groups involved in running. If you just went out and ran down the road continuously for as long as possible your leg muscles would eventually stiffen up, you would get cramp, you would have to stop, and you would have difficulty in walking for several days afterwards. The reasons lie partly in the transport system (the blood) and partly in the chemistry of the muscle fibres themselves — they cannot go on contracting regularly for three or four hours.

There is a third factor in endurance, which only applies to marathon events — this is the carbohydrate reserve. We normally have enough in our energy reserves, in the blood, the muscles and the liver, to last from one-and-a-half to two hours of maximum effort. When these reserves run low the body switches over to using our fat reserves, which causes a sharp decrease in pace (see

Chapter 7 — Hitting the Wall). Part of our training strategy must be to increase the reserves.

Speed may not seem very important to a marathon runner, but however slowly you expect to run, an increase in basic speed will help you improve. Speed in distance running depends mainly on the ability of your heart, arteries and veins (cardiovascular system) to take oxygen to the muscles and get rid of waste products. This means you need a strong heart and a rich blood supply in the working muscles. The development of these capillaries in the muscles is what is known as 'aerobic' training. It takes place when you are working at well below your maximum capacity. At the same time the heart muscle gets stronger and the chemical systems in the muscle fibres become more efficient at handling oxygen.

Speed for the marathon runner does not mean the same thing as speed for the sprinter, who does a lot of his training at 90-100% of his maximum speed. Our training will be a lot slower, around 60-70% of maximum, but still some will be faster than others, and so will be called 'speed work'. On the overload principle, if we train the body to run a little faster than is comfortable, it will adjust to cope with that load, and improvement in basic running speed will occur. This should have already started to take place in your basic jogging programme, and it will continue. Your best mile time may improve from, say, nine minutes to under seven minutes. If you are hoping to run a marathon at a speed of nine minutes per mile, this means that you will have plenty in hand, whereas before the improvement you would be attempting to maintain your maximum mile pace for the whole 26 miles — an obvious impossibility.

Training methods and how they affect you

The majority of the marathon runner's training has always been steady running at a slow pace. As this is what you are going to be doing in a race, it is the logical thing to do, but the questions remain: How far to run? How fast? How often? An experienced runner can judge his speed, in terms of minutes per mile, to within 15 seconds, but for beginners I will use three paces.

Slow pace, as used by those in the LSD school of training, (Long Slow Distance), means a pace which is very easy. The guide is that you should be able to carry on a normal conversation at slow pace. The actual speed is between seven and 10 minutes per mile, depending on your ability.

Moderate or steady pace means a speed at which you hope to run your marathon, or maybe a little faster if you are running distances of six miles or less. Thus, for a three-hour marathoner, seven-minute miles would be steady speed for a 10 mile run, but on a five or six mile course'steady pace' might be 15 seconds a mile faster — about 40 minutes for six miles.

Fast pace means just that; you should be going as fast as possible over the course, without going to the extremes of a race. This means that you will be running at least 30 seconds a mile faster than your marathon speed, maybe one minute a mile faster.

Slow pace running builds up general endurance and is often used as a recovery session in between harder days. It allows the blood to flow through all the working muscles. It will not stress the heart very much, but it gives considerable cardiovascular benefit and so is useful aerobic training. It will do little for your strength, your speed or special endurance, but it will help boost your carbohydrate reserve if you do it for long enough — at least an hour.

Steady pace running will give you greater cardiovascular benefits, help your speed for a marathon and will build up special endurance. Fast running will do all this, too, to a higher degree. Why, then, do I not suggest that all running be done at as fast a speed as possible? Because fast running imposes considerable stress on you, as do races, and you either have to take long recovery periods between fast days, or risk getting an injury. Nor can you run fast enough for long enough to get the endurance benefits essential to a marathon runner. Nevertheless, I am a firm believer in the value of some fast running in training.

Interval Training

This method has been widely used by international track runners for nearly 50 years, but has not been fully taken advantage of by road runners. It is an excellent way of getting the benefits of fast running, without the risks or the mental strain of trying to run several miles at speed. Its benefits were most strikingly shown by Emil Zatopek when he won the Olympic marathon at his first attempt at the distance. He had been training mainly for the 10 kilometres (6 miles) race, but his interval training enabled him to beat all the marathon specialists. In interval training the idea is to run a short distance, which can be anything from 200 yards to half a mile, at a fast tempo, so that your heart rate goes up to well over twice what it is at rest. (See 'Measuring Improvement'.) There is then an interval in which you walk or jog slowly until your heart rate drops again to between 100 and 120 beats per minute, then you repeat the fast stretch.

A typical interval session for a track runner might be 12 fast runs over 400 metres, with a 400 metre jog in two and a half minutes as the slow interval. For a marathon runner the speed will be less, so the recovery jog can be shorter and the fast stretches longer. For our three-hour marathoner, a good session would be eight bursts of half a mile each, at six-minute-mile speed, with a two-minute jog between each. Some good class marathoners, however, like to include short-distance interval training in their schedules, doing, say, a 300 metre burst 30 times in order to maintain their leg speed and stride length. Interval training does not have to be timed or measured; it can be done on road or grass or on a canal path, once the principles are understood. It does, however, lend itself to measurement, because it is a very precise way of giving a definite training load, and it can be increased gradually, either by doing more bursts or by cutting down the recovery interval.

A very useful variation on formal interval training is the Swedish type of training known as *Fartlek* (speed-play). Here, you go on a run and put in fast stretches (of between 200 yards and 600 yards) when you feel like it, jogging slowly afterwards until you feel recovered. This gives you some of the cardiovascular and special endurance benefits that you get from interval training or fast runs, without putting you under too much mental or physical strain. Whether you like this depends on your temperament. Some people like to be told exactly what to do and others like the freedom of being able to make up their own minds about how hard they are going to train on any particular day. *Fartlek* is useful in the training schedule because it can be hard or easy. It provides a safety margin; if your hard sessions are too hard, you will be able to use the *Fartlek* sessions more for recovery, but if you are not working to the maximum in the hard sessions you can do more useful work in the *Fartlek* and so get full value from the week's training.

The next step up from interval running is repetition training. This is a tough but useful form of fast running, where you run a set course, usually between one and two miles, timing it, and after a fixed period of rest you repeat the timed run. A typical session might be four times one-and-a-half miles, with a six minute rest between each. This is both hard training and a means of measuring your improvement. Your time over this distance is directly dependent on your ability to take up and use oxygen, and the one-and-a-half mile run time is used by many physiologists as the best way of estimating cardiovascular fitness in large numbers of people. Credit for this must go to Dr Kenneth Cooper, founder of the Aerobics movement, who found in experiments with US Air Force personnel that there was a very close correlation between the run time and the maximum oxygen uptake figure, as measured directly. If you run a longer distance, say three miles, other factors come into action, such as your will-power, and local muscular endurance. We would recommend using a road course, in some quiet but well-lit area, because you can use this all the year round, without worrying about the state of the going.

Hill Training

In general, your regular training runs will involve some running up and down hills. If it does not, you should certainly include hill training in your schedule, because you will not be a good marathon runner if you cannot cope with hills. Both uphill and downhill running places extra strain on muscle groups, particularly muscles in the back, abdomen and thighs. If these, and the supporting muscles, are unaccustomed to hills, they may let you down at some crucial point. Quite apart from that, hill training has a lot to recommend it. It builds up leg strength, it places increased strain on your cardiovascular system and it is a tremendous confidence booster. When you start training, hills really destroy you. You creep up them, wondering whether you dare run, then wondering whether walking would be faster, then wondering whether you can even keep walking. After a few months you will find yourself running up the same slopes without distress.

Provided you don't start off too rashly, hills can be conquered. The hill that once terrified you becomes your servant, a useful training aid. The secret is to start with little hills and work up. A typical session in the early stages might be run six times up a 50-foot high hill, with a gradient of about one in 10, at the end of a steady run. As weeks go by you increase the number of repetitions, or the height of the hill, until you can run 10 times up a 100-foot hill. It is challenging, and gives variety to your training.

Resistance Work

This includes such things as running through sand, over ploughed fields, running in heavy boots or with a weighted jacket. Because it adds to the load, this type of training does build leg power, but it is only of limited use to marathon runners. Middle distance runners often use these methods to give an extra dimension of toughness to their track training. For marathon runners it has the disadvantage of tending to upset the smooth economical running action that should always be cultivated. We do not recommend it for the novice marathoner. It may suit those who have a background of cross-country running and are used to that kind of work, but for a beginner it is more likely to lead to injury than improvement.

Circuit Training

This involves a fixed pattern of exercises and light weight training. Sports clubs often put on circuit training sessions during winter evenings, and for the average sportsman it is a very good way of acquiring an improvement in all-round fitness, including muscular strength in all groups, co-ordination, some cardiovascular improvement and some endurance. It also has the advantage that you will have like-minded people to train with and someone to keep an eye on your progress. Useful in the first few months of training, but as you become more marathon-oriented you will find that you need the time for running.

Weight Training

A lot of athletes use weights as part of their training; quite distinct from weight lifting and body building, which are sports in their own right. Weight training is useful for improving strength and endurance in specific muscle groups, and some of the top class marathon runners do use it, but most do not, for the following reasons: firstly, you need to know exactly what you are doing, otherwise it may do more harm than good; secondly, it involves a lot of time, unless you have weights readily available; and thirdly, most runners prefer the freedom of the open road to the claustrophobic gymnasium atmosphere. We would suggest that weight training might be brought in for a short time in the build-up phase of the second year's training. It is difficult to combine weight training with high mileage training until you have tried each separately and assessed the benefits to you individually. Most types of physique probably have enough muscle bulk anyway — long distance runners need to carry as little extra weight as possible, and that weight should be concentrated in the muscle groups doing the most work: thighs, calves and hips.

Exercises

Remember that for runners, running comes first and nothing will replace the value of many hours of running per week. Exercises should, however, become a regular part of the weekly routine, because they will improve your chances of avoiding injury. They can be divided into three types.

Loosening exercises are for maintaining your normal range of movement. They should not be painful, but each set of joints should be loosened in turn — neck, shoulders, hips, knees and ankles. You should be warm before you start, and keep yourself warm by moving from one exercise to another. A set of loosening exercises was provided in Chapter 3. These should be regarded as part of your work-out before each run. If possible, you should then go on to the stretching and strengthening exercises detailed below. Certainly, you should go through the whole routine at least twice a week.

Sometimes, though, time may not permit; in this case, start running after the loosening exercises but remember to take the first quarter of a mile steadily. When undertaking a 'quality' session, many people jog a short distance then do a few repetition strides at 75 per cent effort over 50 yards before embarking o nthe session proper. This ensures that you are warmed up thoroughly.

When doing the full exercise session, you come next to the stretching exercises. Here you are trying to increase your range of movement. Greater range of movement will give you perhaps an extra inch or so on your stride, with no increased effort, or it may help you to get in more strides per minute. In a marathon you run about 1000 strides per mile, so an extra inch on your stride length will give you an advantage of 38 yards a mile, or over 700 yards in a marathon. If you can speed up your striding rate without loss of stride length, so that you get in two more strides per minute (the normal rate is between 150 and 200 strides a minute, depending on your build), you will gain about 20 yards per miles. This can happen, because in many runners stiffness in joints and inactive muscles interferes with your running action. You may be doing work in stretching 'unwilling' muscles, work which should be employed in moving you along faster.

Stretching Exercises

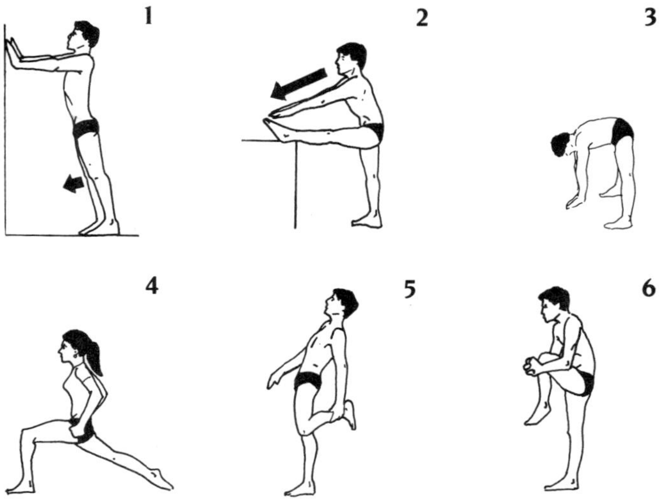

1. **Calf stretch.** Stand facing a wall, so that your finger tips can almost reach it when your arms are outstretched. Keeping your heels firmly on the floor, lean forwards, with your hands resting on the wall, so that your calf muscles are slightly stretched. Hold the position for 30 seconds, then lean further to get a little extra stretch.
2. **Bar stretch** (for hamstrings). Stand facing a table, desk or 3 foot bar. Raise your right leg and place the heel on the table, then lean forward from the waist. Allow 30 seconds plus on each leg.
3. **Inner thigh.** Stand with feet wide apart and lean forward so that you are pushing the palms of your hands towards the floor. Hold for 30 seconds, but try to remain relaxed and continue breathing.

4. **Runner's stretch** (groin). Place the left foot forward and push the right foot back behind you. Push your seat nearer the ground, bending your left leg. Hold the stretch as before, 30 seconds per leg.
5. **Quadriceps pull.** Standing on your right leg, grasp your left ankle in your left hand and pull it up under you until you feel the stretch in the front of the thigh. Repeat with other leg.
6. **Gluteal pull** (seat muscles). Standing on your right leg, raise your left knee towards your chest. Put both hands around the knee and pull it up until you feel the pull on the back of the thigh. Repeat with other leg.

Strengthening Exercises

To be done daily in training but *not* in the pre-race warm-up.

1. **Sit-ups** (back and abdominal muscles). Lying on back, with feet straight out and hands behind back. Aim at 20 sit-ups a day, or as many as you can do in 30 seconds.
2. **Leg raising** (abdominals). Lie on your back with your feet straight out in front. Raise both feet about 18 inches off the floor, hold for 10 seconds, then lower. Repeat four to six times.
3. **Back extension.** Lie face down, then try to raise your chest and your feet off the floor. Hold for 10 seconds, then lower. Repeat four to six times.
4. **Calf raise.** Stand with front half of feet on a step and your heels hanging over the edge. Lower your heels, then raise yourself onto your toes. Repeat 20 to 40 times.

Progressive Training Schedules

How to use the schedules:

1. Select Year One. Year Two or Year Three, according to your ambitions.
2. Go through the first two-week schedule without pushing hard at any point, and doing the minimum mileage indicated.
3. Repeat the first two-week session, using the lowest number of miles indicated each time, but working moderately hard on the hard sessions and taking the easy sesions very easily indeed. Record your performances, times, number of repetitions and how you feel after each day.
4. Provided that you complete the two-week session without undue strain you can move up to the next. This should take you to the end of the progressive schedules in a minimum time of 14 weeks. From then on follow the programme of the final two weeks until you are ready for the two-week 'Race Preparation' session. If you find that completing the last two-week schedule left you tired, or if you failed to complete the harder sessions, repeat that two-week programme before moving up to the next.

Measuring Improvement

First, you must keep a daily log. Without a training and racing diary, you cannot see your pattern, and so cannot see clearly the reasons for your success or failure. The log should record the total distance run, the distance and time, if known, of the fast stretches, the weather conditions and, in particular, your reaction to the day's training. This should be done on the actual day — it is remarkable how time can put a gloss over your immediate reactions. It is said that the Eskimos have 40 different words for snow, because snow plays such a vital role in their daily lives. In the same way, there is an almost infinite range of ways of describing a run. The exercise physiologists use a one to 20 scale of 'perceived effort', ranging from one, which is barely perceptible effort to 20 which is the outermost limit of human endurance, reached only occasionally in a season by runners at national level. You can use this, or you can use a verbal range, such as: fairly easy — moderately hard — quite hard — good and hard — hard but tolerable — very hard — flat out. This is important, because when you look back in your diary it will tell you whether you have been over- or under-stressing yourself in a particular period, and this may give a clue to your performance. Alternatively, when you see that you have run your 10-mile lap in 66 minutes, in cold, wet, weather, and you put down 'moderately hard', it is very heartening to read that three months before you had run the same course in the same time, but in ideal conditions, and had noted it as 'hard work, tired'. Record your training companions, if any, as well, because that can make a big difference to your performance on long runs.

The other essential point, in our view, is the need for regular 'measurement sessions'. These may be straight runs or interval sessions, but they should be done in the same place, preferably at the same time of day, under the same conditions. Different measurement sessions can be used to test your improvement in certain factors. We suggest the following:

For speed: one to one-and-a-half mile road course, or six laps on the track.

For oxygen intake and special endurance (i.e., whether your leg muscles can stand a fast continuous pace): four to six mile road loop.

For general endurance: time for steady, unpressured run round 15 mile loop.

It is *not* a good idea to make every training session a time trial. There are often times, when you are training hard, when your physical condition takes a dip down; any good runner knows this, and knows that he has to go through these tough times in order to make real progress, but for the beginner it may be thoroughly upsetting to find that in the fourth month of hard training he is running a course slower than in the second month. Record your times, certainly, but don't stake your reputation on every run. One trial a week is plenty, and if you are racing, use the race as the true judge of your fitness.

First Year Marathon Programme

We are assuming that you have a background of regular jogging or fitness running. You have got used to going out for a run about four times a week, and you have been running about 15 to 20 miles a week for the month before starting this plan. Try to keep to the same routine for your marathon training, choosing times and places to run which fit in with your daily life. If there is too much conflict, something or someone will eventually crack, which is not the object of the training. You want to run a marathon — that is good, but running should enrich your life, not restrict it. This programme should enable the novice marathoner to break four hours, if he or she is not too old or decrepit.

Weeks One and Two.
Mileage: 25 miles a week.
Day One: 5 miles steady. Record time.
Day Two: 4 miles. Start slow, finish fast.
Day Three: 4 miles on grass.
Day Four: 7 miles, slow pace. Record time.
Day Five: Rest.
Day Six: 4 miles approx., slow, checking the hill training area.
Day Seven: Rest.

During the second week, follow the same programme, but make the second day a fast timed run and do not record the time for the steady 5 miles. Record all your runs in your training diary. The exact distances of each run are not vital, but keeping accurate records for your regular courses is important.

Weeks Three and Four.
Mileage: 25-30 miles per week.
Day One: 6 miles steady. Record time.
Day Two: 5 miles fast. Record time.
Day Three: 4 miles easy on grass.
Day Four: Rest.
Day Five: 1 mile jog, 8 × 100m uphill (1 minute recovery), 2 miles slow.
Day Six: Rest.
Day Seven: 8 miles slow pace.

During the second week, maintain the same effort level but put in a slow 2 mile jog after the hard sessions on Days Two and Five.

Weeks Five and Six.
Mileage: 28-33 miles per week.
Day One: 5 miles easy *Fartlek*.
Day Two: 6 miles fast. Record time.
Day Three: 4 miles easy on grass.
Day Four: Rest.
Day Five: 2 miles jog. 12 × 100m uphill (1 minute recovery), 2 miles slow.
Day Six: Rest.
Day Seven: 10 miles slow. Record time.
During the second week, hold the effort at the same level. We have introduced two increases in quality, plus extra distance on the long slow run.

Weeks Seven and Eight.
Mileage: 30-35 miles a week.
Day One: 1 mile easy, then 4 miles of interval training, running 1 minute fast, followed by 2 minutes jogging. 1 mile easy to complete 6 miles.
Day Two: 5 miles steady.
Day Three: 4 miles easy on grass.
Day Four: Rest.
Day Five: 1 mile warm-up. 6 miles steady. Record time.
Day Six: Rest.
Day Seven: 10 miles slow-steady. Record time.
During the second week, replace the interval training session with a hill session as in Week Six. Time yourself over either your five-mile or six-mile course and try to improve your time.

Week Nine.
Mileage: 40 miles approx.
Day One: 5 or 6 miles steady.
Day Two: 8 miles steady (same pace as day one).
Day Three: 4 miles easy on grass.
Day Four: 5 miles *Fartlek* or intervals (as Week Seven).
Day Five: 5 or 6 miles steady. Record time.
Day Six: Rest.
Day Seven: 10-12 miles slow (to complete 40 in the week).

Week Ten.
Mileage: 32-35 miles.
Day One: 2 miles jog, 15 × 100m uphill, 2 mile run back.
Day Two: 6 miles steady. Record time.
Day Three: 4 miles easy on grass.
Day Four: 1 mile easy, 1 mile fast, 5 mins rest, 1 mile fast, 2 mile jog. Record mile times.
Day Five: 5 miles easy.
Day Six: Rest.
Day Seven: 7-10 miles, starting slow, finishing steady.

Week Eleven.
Mileage: 40 miles
Day One: 5 miles *Fartlek* or intervals.
Day Two: 10 miles steady. Record time.
Day Three: 4 miles easy on grass.
Day Four: 5 miles steady.
Day Five: Rest.
Day Six: 13 miles, starting easy, finishing steady.
Day Seven: 3 miles easy on grass.

Week Twelve.
Mileage: 35-40 miles.
Day One: 5 miles, steady-fast, record time.
Day Two: 8-10 miles steady.
Day Three: 3-5 miles jogging and striding.
Day Four: 1 mile jog, 3 × 1 mile fast (as Week Ten), 1 mile jog.
Day Five: 4 miles easy on grass.
Day Six: Rest.
Day Seven: 10 miles steady. Record time.

Continued Progression

Everyone has to work out their own pattern and this pattern will have to take into account the kind of running which suits their temperament and the demands on their time. When you are under strain, steady or slow continuous running is the best kind of training. If, on the other hand, your work is sedentary and you need some stimulus, the high pressure training of the repetition miles, hill climbs or interval training may suit you. Remember that there are many ways of improving, and you are more likely to keep up your training if it fits in with your way of life rather than clashing with it.

So far, the schedule has taken you through only 12 weeks, and the mileage has built up to double what it used to be. We would suggest that you consolidate at around 40 miles a week, or 45 at the maximum. The vital sessions in the last weeks before the race are the steady runs over 10-12 miles. You should try to get into double figures for five days in every two-week period. There is a rule-of-thumb in the running world which says that the maximum distance you can run in one go is about three times your regular training distance. If your long runs are only eight miles, your chances of covering the full 26 in a race are slim, but if you are used to 10, and can occasionally run a half-marathon in training, you will make it.

The 12 week schedule contains two basic patterns, one as in Week Ten, with hills and repetitions, and one as in Week Eleven, where the emphasis is on the long runs. For the sake of variety, we recommend alternating the two patterns.

After repeating Weeks Ten, Eleven and Twelve, the next step is to increase the mileage gradually, if you have the time, by adding one or two miles to two of the longer runs, and an extra mile in the repetition series. If you cannot afford any more time, stay on the 40-miles a week session, concentrating on improving times, but try to increase the distance of your occasional races, running half-marathons or 15-mile races, rather than 10 kilometre races.

Second Year Marathon Programme

If you have been bitten sufficiently hard by the marathon bug continue to the second year of training. We are assuming that you have had several months of running about 40 miles a week, perhaps going up to 50 miles at times, and that you have got used to putting in some good quality sessions from time to time. You have probably run at least two full marathons, the first tentatively, taking it very slowly, and finishing in under four hours, and the second with more determination, starting well but finishing very tired. You have decided that you could run something under three hours 30 minutes, perhaps even close to three hours, if you had the right training. This is where you start. The principle is the same — that we are going to work up to a regular 60 miles a week, but 60 miles of quality training, not just jogging along. This will take up less time and get you into better condition than far more time spent on long slow runs. You should be thinking of 7 mins to 7 mins 30 as your 'steady' miling speed.

Weeks One and Two.

Mileage: 45-50 miles a week.

Day One: 10-11 miles slow.

Day Two: 6-8 miles, starting slow, finishing fast.

Day Three: On grass or path, 5-7 miles jogging and striding.

Day Four: Run out to hills, 3-4 miles, unpressured, on hills, jog back.

Day Five: Rest.

Day Six: 2 mile warm-up, then 6 miles steady. Record time.

Day Seven: 3-4 miles slow in morning, 6-8 steady in evening.

Progression:

If you find that you are putting in the increased mileage without undue strain, and managing to live a normal life-style, go on to Week Three. If you have been unable to run 45 miles, or found it hard, repeat the weeks until this can be run without strain.

Weeks Three and Four.

Mileage: 50-55 miles a week.

Day One: 11-14 miles, slow pace.

Day Two: 2-mile jog. 8 × 300 yds uphill course, untimed, jog back to recover. 2-4 miles steady.

Day Three: On grass or paths, 6-8 miles *Fartlek*.

Day Four: Rest or slow 2 mile jog.

Day Five: 1 mile easy, 5-7 miles steady (timed), jog down.

Day Six: Easy 5-6 miles, with a little striding.

Day Seven: Warm-up. Race or repetition running: 5 × 1 mile at fast pace (5 mins recovery). Record times.

Progression:

We are introducing two new sessions, the long hills, and the repetition miles (which need not be exact). Both these sessions should be done at a brisk tempo, that is, considerably faster than your marathon miling speed. In the first week, run them easily, but record the number you achieve, and the times of your repetition runs. In the following week, put in a little more effort and establish a baseline from which you can aim to improve. Repeat this two weeks if you feel that it took a lot of adjusting to.

Weeks Five and Six.
Mileage: 50-60 miles a week.
Day One: 10-15 miles steady. Record time.
Day Two: Hill training as Week Three or 15 × 200 yds striding, following a brisk 4 miles.
Day Three: Warm-up. Steady 6-8 miles at good marathon pace (timed).
Day Four: On grass or paths, 5-7 miles, starting slow, finishing fast.
Day Five: 6-8 miles *Fartlek* or Intervals as in Year One, Week Seven.
Day Six: Rest or slow 3-mile jog.
Day Seven: Warm-up. Race or repetition miles (5 mins recovery). Record time and aim to improve.

Progression:
This is a mid-point session where you have to get used to running up to 60 miles a week, including quality sessions. In alternate weeks concentrate on firstly, doing the fast running fast and, secondly, getting in the miles and not worrying too much about the quality. When you can manage 60 a week *without* having to cut down on the quality, you are ready to move on. You are the one who can sense how fast you should run, and the timed session over about five miles will be a good estimate of your fitness.

Weeks Seven and Eight.
Mileage: 55-60 miles a week.
Day One: 13-16 miles, slow to steady pace. Record time.
Day Two: Hill running or 20 × 200 yds striding, following 3-4 miles steady.
Day Three: On grass or paths, 5-7 miles unpressured.
Day Four: Warm-up 1 mile. 10-12 at steady pace. (Record time.)
Day Five: 6-8 miles *Fartlek*.
Day Six: Rest or easy 3 miles.

Day Seven: Warm-up. Race or repetitions: 2 × 2 miles fast (8 mins recovery). Record time.

Progression:
We are now concentrating on the two long runs a week, while maintaining all the other facets of our training on Days Two, Five and Seven. Do not try to improve on every session each week. This is the time for aiming for distance and holding your ground in the other sessions. It is dangerous to try to improve too many things at once.

Weeks Nine and Ten.
Mileage: 60 miles a week.
Day One: 13-16 miles slow to steady. Record time.
Day Two: Warm-up 1 mile. 5 miles good speed, untimed.
Day Three: 5-7 miles on grass, including 8 × 200 yds striding.
Day Four: 13 miles at marathon speed, starting slowly.
Day Five: Long warm-up. 6-8 miles *Fartlek*.
Day Six: Rest or 3 mile jog.
Day Seven: Race or 3 × 2 miles repetition (5 mins recovery).

Weeks Eleven and Twelve. Two-week race preparation.*
Day One: 1 mile warm-up. Half-marathon, steady speed, timed.
Day Two: Run to hills. Hill session as Week Seven, run back.
Day Three: 5-7 miles jogging and striding on grass.
Day Four: Warm-up. Fast run, timed, over 5-6 mile course.
Day Five: Rest or easy jog.
Day Six: Race warm-up. 2 hour steady run.
Day Seven: 3 mile slow jog on grass, plus stretching.
Day Eight: 8 miles *Fartlek*, starting slowly.
Day Nine: Race warm-up. 10 miles at marathon pace.
Day Ten: 5-6 miles jogging and striding on grass.
Day Eleven: Race warm-up, 2 miles slow, 5 miles at marathon pace.
Day Twelve:
Day Thirteen: 2 days rest or light jogging.
Day Fourteen: The Marathon Race.

*See p.122 for discussion of the pre-race training programme.

Third Year Marathon Programme

This is where the serious runner starts. Without decrying the achievement of the jogger or the over-40 fitness man or woman, for whom finishing a marathon is a personal triumph, it must be said that for a young runner with serious intent, nothing over two hours 50 minutes is worthy of serious consideration. To put it into the context of track running, the 2hrs 45 mins marathon is equivalent to running an 800 metres in about 2 mins 10 secs — not bad for a girl or a veteran, but nothing special for a serious runner. The drawback is the sheer volume of training which needs to be done in order to run a marathon properly.

The schedules given below, like those above, are designed to give the maximum benefit from as little mileage as possible. They are based on the schedules which I trained with in the Sixties, on which I ran 20 miles in 101 minutes. These differ little from the kind of training being done by Salazar and Virgin in the Eighties except in total mileage. Although it may be necessary to go up to 110 or 120 miles a week to reach the 2 hrs 10 level, 80 miles a week should enable you to reach the 2 hrs 30 level, for a young man, or the 2 hrs 50 level for a young woman.

The same schedule can be followed whether you are hoping for 2 hrs 25 — a 5 min 30 mile speed, or a 2 hrs 50, which is a 6 mins 30 mile speed. The times given in the schedules are aimed at a marathon in 2 hrs 35 — a speed of just under 6 minutes a mile. The same principles apply as in the other schedules — we increase our mileage gradually, and as we become used to the mileage we increase the quality of the sessions. In the early stages there are three or four hard sessions a week, but as the race approaches we concentrate on putting the major effort into the two long runs, simulating the stresses of the race.

Weeks One and Two.

Mileage: 65-70 miles a week.

Day One: am. 3 miles steady.
pm. 2 miles slow, 4 miles good speed, 1 mile slow.

Day Two: am. 3 miles slow.
pm. Run out to hills, 30 minutes trying out different hill runs, run back, (6 miles).

Day Three: am. 3 miles slow.
pm. 6 to 8 miles *Fartlek*, grass or paths.
Day Four: am. 3 miles easy.
pm. 10 mile course, steady pace. Record time.
Day Five: 3 mile jog only.
Day Six: Club race, with warm-up and warm-down, or warm-up plus fast run over 4-5 mile course.
Day Seven: Long slow run, 11-14 miles.

Weeks Three and Four.
Mileage: 70-75 miles a week.
Day One: Run out to hills (2 or 3 miles), 10 × 200 yds up a moderate hill (jog down recovery). Run back.
Day Two: 2 miles warming up, then 'road intervals' of 5 × 2 mins fast, 2 mins slow, 5 × 1 min fast, 1 min slow, then 3 miles steady pace.
Day Three: 10 mile course, slow pace.
Day Four: 7-8 miles *Fartlek*, grass, beach or paths.
Day Five: Morning run only.
Day Six: Warm-up and down for either a 10 km road race or 2 × 2 mile time trials (6 mins recovery jog).
Day Seven: Mile warm-up plus stretching, then 13 miles at 6 mins 30 pace. Record time.

Progression:
The first two weeks should not prove hard, but some people might find the change to the routine of training twice a day difficult. If you are going to get in good quality training on four days or more a week, your body must have some gentle running to enable it to recover, and for the blood to flush away the fatigue products from the muscles. This *can* be done in a single training session, but the extra fatigue which comes from making every major session 10 or 12 miles will take more getting used to than the morning jog, and is more likely to lead to injuries. The morning run is entirely therapeutic, and no effort should be made, apart from the initial one of getting out of the front door.

When you have got used to both the double sessions and the quality work-outs of the second schedule you may move on, but it is likely that you will have to repeat Weeks Three and Four at least once before you are confident that you can handle this type of training without getting overtired.

Weeks Five and Six.
Mileage: 70-80 miles a week.
Daily run of three miles every weekday.
Day One: Hill training as in Week Three, Day One or 'road intervals' as in Week Three, Day Two.
Day Two: 10-13 mile run at 6 mins 30 speed.
Day Three: 6-8 miles *Fartlek* on grass or paths.
Day Four: 2 miles easy, then fast timed run (sub-6-minute speed) over 5-6 mile course. Jog down.
Day Five: Morning jog only.
Day Six: Warm-up and race or 3 × 2 miles repetition session. Aim at 5 min 30 pace. (6 mins recovery).
Day Seven: 2 hours slow running. 3 miles of jogging and striding out on grass later in day, if possible.

Weeks Seven and Eight.
Mileage: 75-90 miles.
Daily run of three miles every week day.
Week Seven is a 'quality' week, following the same pattern as Week Five, but putting in a harder 'interval' session instead of *Fartlek* on Day Three and making the Day Four run an eight mile stretch at 5 mins 40 speed per mile.

Week Eight is a mileage week, with three long runs, as well as the morning runs.
Day One: 7-8 miles *Fartlek*, with bursts on hills.
Day Two: 15 miles, starting slow, finishing faster.
Day Three: 5-6 miles jogging and striding on grass.
Day Four: Warm-up, then half marathon, 6 minute mile speed.
Day Five: 5 miles jogging and striding on grass.
Day Six: 2 mile jog, 4 miles good speed, 2 mile jog.
Day Seven: 2 mile warm-up, then 15 miles at marathon speed, and 2 miles very slow at finish. Arrange drinking and clothing as for the race.

Week Nine. **Mileage: 60 miles.**
This is a recuperation week, with morning runs daily, plus easy running and *Fartlek*, five to 10 miles a day, until the next weekend, when the Week Seven quality work can start again. This three week cycle should then be maintained until the two-week 'Race Preparation' begins. Remember that it is always possible to increase your training as the weeks go by, but if you have over-trained and are injured it is much more difficult to get back to normal, so be patient and increase the training load very gradually.

Two Week Race Preparation for a 2 hrs 35 mins Marathon.
Day One: 1 mile warm-up. 12 miles at sub-6-minute pace.
Day Two: 7-8 miles of *Fartlek* or road intervals.
Day Three: Warm-up. 3 × 2 miles repetition at 5 mins 40 secs speed.
Day Four: 6-8 miles of jogging and striding on grass.
Day Five: 2 mile jog. Steady pace, timed over 6 mile course.
Day Six: Rest or easy jog.
Day Seven: 20 mile run, not pushing, 2 hrs 10 - 2 hrs 15 mins.
Day Eight: 3 miles slow jog, stretching.
Day Nine: 3 miles easy, 2 miles at race speed, 2 miles easy.
Day Ten: Long warm-up. Measured 10 miles in 57-58 mins.
Day Eleven: 3-4 miles easy on grass. 2 × 1 mile at race speed.
Day Twelve: Rehearse warm-up and start. Jog 2-3 miles.
Day Thirteen: Jog 2-3 miles, over last part of course, if possible.
Day Fourteen: Warm-up. The Marathon Race.

Discussion
When you reach this point in your training, the whole object is to get yourself into the right condition for race day. Details of what to do on the actual day are dealt with in Chapter 7, but you should arrive at that day eager to run and full of energy, not worn out from over-training. The last two weeks therefore follows the 'hard day—easy day' pattern. At the beginning of the two weeks, the pressure is kept up, and you should be running well, but not to exhaustion. Resting up before the 20 mile run, and after it, should permit you to run the full 20 without feeling that you have gone anywhere near your limit. The only hard session left is the 10 mile

run, four days before the big day. The 10 should not be under pressure. Imagine you are running the first 10 of the marathon — you will still have 16 miles to go after it, so just cruise through it at sub-6-minute mile speed. You should recover quickly from this and with three days of light training left you will be in top form when it matters.

CHAPTER 5

Maintenance

WE HAVE SAID that running should add to your life, not restrict it, but there are bound to be times when your marathon ambitions clash with other aspects of your life. The purpose of this chapter is to minimise the clashes, to help you integrate your training with your daily life. In general, the trained runner is a far more effectve and energetic human being than the normal man or woman — except just after a marathon or a hard training session. The first thing, therefore, is to schedule your week so that you can relax for at least a short period of time after the hard sessions — let us say, two weekday evenings and sometime at the weekend. The schedules in the last chapter are listed as Day One to Day Seven, but it does not matter which order you do them in, as long as they are all done in a week, and as long as all the hard sessions do not come together. The other runs — the easy running on grass, the steady untimed run or the *Fartlek*, will have to be fitted into your working day as best you can.

You should not be a slave to your schedule — that way you will just become a running bore. Apart from those special occasions when you have to put running first, the use of a little commonsense will enable you to maintain the equilibrium which is the secret of continued progress. The equilibrium is a healthy balance of rest and exercise. You have to balance the things which tire you against the things which restore you. The best way to do this is to draw up a balance sheet of daily activities, distinguishing between the things which are mentally tiring, without actually taking much physical energy, and those things which are physically tiring and might therefore be considered as part of your daily exercise programme. It often happens that those activities which are the most tiring physically are the most relaxing mentally.

Thus, if your day goes: Walk to station, train into city, walk to office, sit in office, out to lunch, visit business contact, walk to station, catch train home, work in garden, then the only parts of the day which are going to help you to get fit are the walking periods. If these are longish walks, done at a brisk speed, they will help to lay the ground for your daily running, because fast walking does improve your leg muscles and is certainly better for the heart than no exercise at all. Sitting in a train or going out to lunch may leave you with a sensation of tiredness, but it does nothing else, except maybe cause you to put on weight.

The only activities which are doing you good physically are those which use your muscles, and use them at a fast enough pace to get your heart-lung system going. Walking, jogging, cycling, manual labour can all contribute something in the way of endurance training. A man who is spending an hour a day pushing barrows of earth around his garden, or an hour trotting about between buildings on a factory site, is probably adding 20 miles a week to his training schedule, compared to the sedentary man. The sedentary man will have to increase his training to take into account the fact that his muscles are wasting away, through not being used. Rest after effort is fine, and rest before effort is fine, but rest without effort leads to atrophy.

The next question which follows is: 'What is the value of other sports, considered as part of marathon training?' A lot of fun runners are people who enjoy all-round fitness and like to take part in swimming, tennis, badminton and so on. Unless you are participating in a high-intensity sport with the same demands as running, you cannot really count this as part of your fast training, but the hours spent could be counted as endurance training. You can do a conversion, based roughly on the number of calories used per hour in the various different sports.

Running, for a ten stone (140lb/63kg) person, uses about 100 calories per mile — say 800 calories per hour for training. Rowing will use up calories at a slightly faster rate, as will cross-country skiing, but downhill skiing does not use calories at a steady rate for long enough to be regarded as training. Cycling, fast swimming or squash will also have calorie consumption rates approaching those of running, so an hour spent on one of those could be worth at least 45 minutes of running, interms of general endurance. If, however, you swim or play squash more than once a week, the value for marathon training diminishes, because the exercise is not specific enough to educate your muscles into the habits of a runner. If you are running regularly for 50 miles a week or more, you can count your other sports as endurance training, but if you are spending two days a week on other sports without running, the value of those other sports declines. On the other hand, something which closely resembles your marathon running can be counted in full. For example, two hours hard cycling, or a five-mile walk-jog after you have missed your bus, or even two hours of disco dancing. It is the usage of heart, lungs and muscles which counts, particularly leg muscles.

If disco dancing actually counts as training, what about other things normally listed among the vices — tobacco, alcohol, drugs and sex? The answer does not lie in giving up all the things you enjoy — you are trying to be a marathon runner, not a monk.

Alcohol

One of the surprising things about training continuously is that your body makes its own rules and the craving for some of the things you thought you needed often vanishes. You become less dependent on drink and cigarettes, and if you over-indulge you will feel the after-effects next day. However, if you feel like a drink, have one. The human liver is well able to break down alcohol, as lng as the level does not rise too high, and four pints of beer or a bottle of wine can be consumed every day without ill effects. Avoid drinking before training, though — it does slow you down. Some people have been tempted to have an alcoholic drink in the latter part of a marathon race. The results are usually disastrous; you may get a brief stimulus, but this will leave you more tired and dehydrated than before.

The best time to drink is after the race, and the best thing to drink is a light beer. It tastes good and it puts back the fluid you have lost in the race as well as the salts. The small amount of alcohol, on an empty stomach, produces, in my experience a pleasant pain-killing effect. But I have known it to make other people sick. You just have to experiment.

Smoking

With tobacco, there is no doubt that smoking cuts down your oxygen intake. The smoke, when inhaled, stops the little hairs of the trachea lining from functioning normally. This may lead to irritation of the lung passages. More seriously, the effect of tobacco on the alveoli of the lung is to reduce the amount of oxygen you can take in. How much is harmful? One cigarette a day is not going to have a noticeable effect, but 20 a day will. As with alcohol, the body is able to cope with the harmful effects as long as you give at a chance. Thus, if you normally smoke two or three cigarettes in an evening, they don't do much harm, and if you happen to go to a party and smoke eight or ten you might find it affects your training for the next day or two.

Not so much is known about the effects on runners of smoking marijuana, but we would put it into the same category as strong drink, in that it effects normal judgement and slows you down. Like tobacco, it will also impair lung function. On the other hand, if you are used to smoking occasionally, it is not going to prevent you improving your fitness level, and as you become more self-reliant as a runner you may well find that you depend less on any kind of drug.

Sex

Sex is different, in that it is a normal human activity, not in any way harmful. The idea that sex ruins sports performances dates from the days of professional boxing, when the boxer was regarded as some sort of animal who would abandon training and indulge in orgies if he were not kept in monastic conditions. There may be some truth in the idea that the competitive instinct is sublimated sexual drive, and hence frustrated men, and women too, run faster, but we are talking of a whole lifestyle, and our goal is the fully developed human being, the complete person. Sex is only incompatible with running if it interferes seriously with sleep.

Sleep

Sleep is important. Rest is part of the training process and if you do not get enough sleep you will not derive the benefit from your training. This is where the sense of equilibrium comes in. When you are training hard you cannot afford many late nights, but the body works on a weekly budget, and you can afford to have one late night a week without doing any harm to the training. How late is late? Eight hours of sleep are needed when you are training seriously, and perhaps nine hours after a really long run. Young runners, under 21, may need a little longer.

Illness and Injuries

If you doubt that running is addictive, observe the behaviour of an injured runner and you will see a whole series of withdrawal symptoms: displacement activities, over-compensation, hypochondria and neurasthenia. The only thing he wants to do is get back running, but experience tells us that this is not always the best thing to do. The guidelines should be:

1. If you are definitely ill, i.e. you have an infection, a fever, or food poisoning, do not run at all.
2. If you are just feeling unwell, either rest or have a short easy jog.
3. If you have a leg injury, even a slight strain, stop that day's training, cool the injured area with ice or cold water and keep weight off it.
4. The day after an injury, try walking a mile before attempting to jog. If you can walk and jog a mile without pain you can then proceed, cautiously, into your training.
5. If the injury does not respond to three days of this rest/walk/jog treatment, see a doctor, preferably one who is familiar with sports injuries, or a physiotherapist with a known record of treating runners. Follow professional advice to the letter, without trying to introduce your own remedies at the same time. If you feel that your doctor does not know enough about running injuries, or has no sympathy with them, there are now a number of sports injuries clinics to which you can be referred. There is a list of National Health hospitals in Britain which have departments catering specifically for the type of injury a runner is likely to receive in Chapter 9. If in doubt you should consult fellow runners or seek advice at a running club.

How to avoid injuries

The first rule is to have a planned progressive training schedule — which you now have — and the second rule is to stick to it. Do not be persuaded into running a fast five miles on the road with somebody faster, when you are feeling stiff from a hard session the previous day. The schedules we have given you are designed to keep you from running on the road every day of the week. The vast improvement in the quality of training shoes has decreased the chances of stress injuries, but it is still good policy to break up your road running by training on soft going twice a week. There are people who train on the road all the time and get away with it, but the human frame was not designed for hard roads.

Choosing the right training and racing shoes has already been dealt with in Chapter 3, but you can further protect yourself by having a pair of walking boots. When the weather is too cold and the road too icy for serious running, you can derive useful exercise from putting on a thick track suit and a protective outer shell and going for a steady jog in boots. This prevents you from injuring yourself running on frozen ground or slipping on the ice. The boots will also come in useful if you are suffering from the beginnings of 'shin splints' or Achilles tendon strain, because when you are told to stop running, you can still walk safely in boots without aggravating the injury.

This is not the place to list all the injuries you can suffer through running; the effect would be depressing and misleading. Although you hear about 'shin splints', runner's knees, and so on, the runner who trains sensibly will seldom have problems unless he has some basic problem such as unequal leg length. As the most experienced of runners amongst the authors I have raced between 40 and 50 times a year for over 10 years, at national and international level, and have only missed two races through injury. The guidelines to avoiding injury are simple, but they must be adhered to.

1. Carry out your stretching and loosening exercises before running.
2. By using protective clothing and warming up thoroughly, make sure that your muscles are properly warm before you start fast running.
3. After your hard training, 'warm down' for five minutes. This will maintain the blood flow through your muscles and flush away waste products.
4. After warming down, shower and change as soon as possible. If this cannot be done, put on plenty of warm clothing and keep moving gently to avoid stiffness.

5. Never run hard on stiff muscles. Stiffness is a natural protection against overuse, and if you push any harder you will pull a muscle. Jog slowly until the discomfort has gone.
6. When you start a new type of training, say intervals on the track, treat the first session as a gentle try-out. Running in different shoes or on different surfaces is the most frequent cause of injury, so always make change-overs gently.
7. Do not go on running in old, worn-out or borrowed shoes.

Food and Drink

More nonsense is written about this than any other topic in the fitness spectrum. 'We are what we eat' is as meaningless a generalisation as 'seeing is believing'. We are not what we eat. The human is an omnivore, having a digestive system which can cope with an enormous range of foods. These foods are broken down into a fairly small number of simple 'building-blocks' — sugars, fatty acids, glycerol, amino-acids, vitamins, minerals and water. These raw materials are then passed around in the blood stream so that they may be used in the cells, stored (in some cases) or broken down and excreted.

How we develop depends on our age, our genetic nature and our activity or lack of it. Lack of the right food can prevent us reaching our genetic potential, but excess quantities of the right food will not make us exceed our potential. The best evidence for this view comes from looking at people from different parts of the world. In the marathon we see equally good performances by the Japanese, on a rice and fish diet, by Mexicans on a maize, eggs and beans diet, by Bill Rodgers on a 'junk food' diet and by many others on a vegetarian diet.

The important components in a runner's diet are Regularity, Digestibility, Balance and Energy Content. Regularity is important because as runners we burn up energy faster than most, and we do not have the fat reserves of non-runners. Three meals a day are essential, otherwise you will not be able to get the calorie content and the balance into your daily eating. The size of the meal depends on your training routine, but for the person who trains after work each of the meals should be substantial. If you are going to have a 10-mile run at six o'clock and eat at 7.45, you need something more substantial than a snack lunch between breakfast and supper. If you run during your lunch hour you probably won't have either the time or the inclination for a large lunch and you may have a tea-time snack to make up for it. This is fine as long as your daily diet meets the Balance requirements. Regular moderate meals are better than a single blow-out in the evenings, which may lead to indigestion

Digestibility should not really be a problem, but remember that some foods do remain a long time in the stomach, particularly fried foods and raw foods, and you must allow sufficient time for the stomach to be emptied before hard training. Liquid meals, such as soup, or high carbohydrate meals, such as honey sandwiches or pancakes with syrup, will be digested quickly. Before a race your digestion rate is considerably slowed down, so you should eat your last meal at least three hours beforehand. If you are running a marathon in the morning, be sure you have a good carbohydrate breakfast over three hours beforehand. It is a bad mistake to miss breakfast at any time, but particularly on the morning of a race.

In the long term it is the Balance of your diet which matters most. You must have sufficient Energy Content to satisfy the calorie demands of your training, and enough of the other essentials of diet to make sure that you don't suffer from any deficiencies.

You may have noticed that young people eat enormous quantities of food without putting on weight. This is because, apart from using up a lot of energy, they have an 'appestat' which ensures that, if they eat too much, their metabolic rate speeds up and the excess energy food is 'burned up'. The same process applies to most runners. Their continual activity keeps the appestat in operation long after it has ceased to function in normal people of their age.

If you are running 50 miles a week you are burning up over 5,000 calories a week, on top of your usual consumption. Someone with a sedentary job who takes up marathon running may well be increasing their daily consumption of calories by 20 or 25 per cent. Their food consumption need not go up by this amount, because most of us eat rather more than we need anyway, but a 10 per cent increase in energy foods is not unreasonable. If you are burning up more than you eat you will gradually use up your body fat, but don't expect very rapid results — you need to run 20 miles or more to take off a pound of fat.

It is certainly worth keeping a check on your body weight, to discover any changes, but a weekly check-up is sufficient. In any one day your weight will vary by two or three pounds, depending on whether you weigh yourself before or after meals and before or after training. On a long run you can lose two pounds through sweating, but most of that will be put back as drink in the next few hours. If you weigh yourself at the same time each week, you will soon see whether your eating and your running match up.

The balanced diet requires carbohydrates, fats, proteins, vitamins, minerals and water, and every meal you eat should contain all these groups. Fats are not bad for you — they are essentials — and they will only be damaging to those people who eat too much and exercise too little. Carbohydrates, such as bread, maize, potatoes, rice, pasta, form the basis of most human diets, and there is usually enough fat involved in the preparation — butter, cooking oil, etc., for you to get your requirements without worrying.

Do runners need extra protein? Possibly, when they increase their training load, because fibres are being broken down and repaired, but the normal requirement is less than four ounces (100 grams) a day, and the Ethiopians manage to run well on very little animal protein, so large steaks won't make you run faster.

On the matter of vitamins and minerals, it is more difficult to be precise. If your daily diet always includes fresh fruit, salad or green vegetable, milk, eggs and wholemeal bread, you will be getting all you need. If you are worried about this, try putting yourself on a month-long course of multi-vitamins plus iron, and see if it affects your form. People who are forced to eat out a lot, and to eat snack meals or junk food would be well advised to take vitamin pills regularly.

Drinking plenty of fluid is to be recommended, because runners use a considerable amount of liquid when sweating.

Water is as good as anything, but there is no reason why you should not drink it in the form of tea, milk, beer, lemonade or orange juice. Liquids are absorbed most easily, so after a long run a sweet drink will be the most reviving. Proprietary drinks such as Staminade or Gatorade are a convenient source, but you can make your own more cheaply, if you wish.

We will deal with specialist drinks and the question of pre-race diet ('carbo-loading' etc.) and refreshment/replenishment during the race in Chapter 7.

In food and drink, as in training, let your body tell you what it wants. Common-sense should be your guide. There is no magic potion which is going to turn you into a superhuman immediately, but by care and progressive training you can become a superman or woman and you will be able to do things which were previously quite impossible, and that is most satisfying.

CHAPTER 6

The Racing Programme

Racing will be the last word on your mind at this moment. Finishing might be a better word to sum up your most immediate ambition. Surviving might be another. Indeed, racing is always the last word for the marathon runner; only a few are ever good enough to describe what they do realistically in terms of racing.

For most the only race will be in their own mind against themselves and the clock. Whether they place 100th or 10,000th will depend less on any racing ability than the size of the original field. Whether they finish at all and when will be more significant than where.

But racing is what you are aiming to do, and will be doing the moment you step up to the starting line. Jogging may be an end in itself but training is not a sufficient qualification to be a marathon runner. You have to have run the distance in a competitive situation, and that by any definition is a race. And the only way to achieve that goal is to build a ladder towards it.

The lowest rungs are the training which we have covered in the previous chapters. But above them is the competitive build-up to the marathon itself and then the marathon. That is the racing programme, and it should be planned with as much care as the training before it.

The elite racer, whatever his distance, prepares himself for each season with a few races at distances different to the one in which he intends specialising. An 800 metres runner may sharpen up with the odd 400 metres; the 5,000 metres runner will lead up to it with a mile or two and perhaps a 3,000 metres. A marathon runner similarly will loosen up with under-distance road races.

For the novice, the process is more akin to building stepping stones. Running a marathon before running any other race would be as unwise as making Everest your first mountain. You need to sample the atmosphere of competition at a lower level to be ready for the real thing.

Training will prepare your body. Only running in races can prepare your mind. In competition you will learn your own capacity for racing and your strengths and weaknesses, you will learn about tactics and psychology and even little nuances of the race day.

It would hardly be sensible to turn up for your first marathon so unaware that you wasted precious mental energy worrying about the basics of reporting, collecting your number and where to line up.

Racing is, in any case, what this is all about, what separates the jogger from the runner perhaps. Running without racing is like a cricketer who only plays in the nets. It might improve his ability and his fitness but in the end it will grind him down mentally.

A race stimulates — it is a lot more fun running a 10 mile road race than just running 10 miles. It will also give you a better appreciation of your continuing improvement.

Once you reach the point where you can run continuously for 30 minutes and can look to the future with some confidence start thinking of your first race. You may be thinking only of that first marathon. Possibly any other race at an intermediate stage will not interest you. There is nothing wrong with that. It can be done that way, and was by many of those who ran their first race of any sort in the first London Marathon.

It is, however, more logical to take a marathon in stages. Before the advent of the people's marathons and fun runs, all marathons demanded qualifying times from a 20 mile race. It was necessary in those days to ensure that nobody ran who would not have a reasonable chance of finishing before every official went home. It had the secondary advantage of ensuring a runner's experience. Even a little bit goes a long way to making that first marathon less awesome.

Many marathons now provide their own stepping stones. The Alan Blatchford Masters and Maidens Marathon, in Guildford in Surrey, offer a 10 mile race in July and a 15 mile race a month before the marathon, and their marathon is definitely in the fun run class, discouraging those who have bettered three hours and encouraging those who may be too anxious for a formal race.

So let's plan a programme of races leading up to the marathon. The first question to dispose of is where you find out when and where races are being held. This is simple as you can take advantage of the great depth of coverage of road race fixtures now available in magazines.

In Britain, *Running* is a monthly magazine which has an events diary listing road races and their organisers month by month. *Athletics Weekly* offers a similar service through its race advertisements. In America, *Runner's World*, which is monthly, gives a tremendous survey state-by-state each month and offers an annual fixture list.

You may have decided by now to join an athletics club. This is not essential. New Amateur Athletic Association rules in England allow you to run as 'unattached' for as long as you choose, although some organisers, such as those of the London Marathon, charge the 'unattached' larger entry fees. But as a member of a club, you will not only have the advantage of your club's own fixture list but may join the Road Runners Club.

The RRC offers a comprehensive list each year, although they concern themselves only with races of 10 miles or more. The American Road Runners Club offers an even wider selection of races.

Failing these approaches, write to your national governing body. Their addresses are at the back of this book. They have to sanction every serious race held within their borders, and that makes their list unimpeachable.

On the subject of national governing bodies, remember that as far as they are concerned those who run in events not sanctioned by them are making themselves ineligible for future sanctioned events. It is a rule honoured more in the breech, and there are an increasing number of races on both sides of the Atlantic, especially among the fun run brigade, which simply do not bother to be sanctioned.

Most will not cause you any trouble. But if you find one offering cash prizes or excessive prizes in kind, take care. You may be putting your future races at risk. Check with your club or area athletic association.

You must also ensure that you are old enough to run a certain distance. Those 18 and over in England and Wales may run any distance. Curiously boys of 17 may only run 15 km (9½ miles) while girls of that age may run 25 km (15 miles) but the AAA are expected to bring their rule up to date soon. Below those ages the distances gradually decrease. In America and Germany there are no such limits.

Once you have done this you can select your own races. I am assuming now, of course, that the training has gone well, you are running regularly and can now see that first marathon on the horizon no more than a few months away. Pick your target. Just as an illustration, we shall say it is the Pony Greater Manchester Marathon in late August. You should have no difficulty entering as there are no time or numerical limits.

Write the marathon at the top of your sheet of paper. Now work backwards. Find a 20 mile race at least four weeks before the marathon, possibly as much as six weeks. You must keep the gaps wide at this stage to allow plenty of recovery time. Three or four weeks before that select a 15 mile race (or 25 km). Then go back over the previous few months and pick out a few 10 mile races. Right at the beginning, if you have started completely from scratch, try a five mile race. The programme could read something like this:

August 23	Greater Manchester Marathon
July 18	Belgrave Harriers 20 mile
June 27	Great North Run (half marathon)
June 7	Michelin 10 (Stoke-on-Trent)
May 24	Ernest Harper 10 mile (Sheffield)
April 25	Herne Hill 10 mile
March 28	Sri Chinmoy 5 miles (London)

The places are irrelevant. They could just as easily be American races. The importance is the spacing between them and their progression. You may wish to race more often, and certainly there is a case for slipping a short race into the schedule a week or so before the marathon as a warm-up.

You should also find a few alternative dates in case you are unavoidably forced to miss one of those scheduled. And don't forget to send off your entries. Most races will not accept entries on the day.

It is as well, too, to have a word with the organiser or somebody within your own club or group who has run the races you choose. Herne Hill's Open 10, which is on our list, is not suitable for a debut 10. It is too tough.

Here again it does help to be a member of the RRC. They operate a standards scheme. Besides being an excellent incentive scheme for improvement, it grades every road race of 10 miles and up.

The RRC scheme is intended to encourage those who will not be among the winners by rewarding and marking their time achievements. To qualify for a first or second class certificate, a runner has to achieve certain times for three different distances (say 10 miles, 15 miles and marathon).

The RRC take into consideration the severity of each course. It is a sort of handicapping system. You only have to consult the RRC Standards List to see whether a particular race is tougher than average.

So the Croxdale 10 has a minute added to its standards over the Worthing 10, and the Belgrave 20 is allowed two minutes longer than the Finchley 20. When it comes to the marathon itself, the RRC rate the Duchy of Cornwall and Isle of Wight marathons the toughest they have yet measured and three minutes tougher than a race such as the Polytechnic Harriers race in Windsor.

For men and women the following standards have been applied by the RRC to British marathons:

	Men				**Women**	
	1st class	2nd	Vet 40+	Vet 50+	1st	2nd
Aberdeen	2:37	3:07	3:12	3:27	3:12	3:44
Barnsley	2:35	3:05	3:10	3:25	3:05	3:42
Cambridge	2:35	3:05	3:10	3:25	3:05	3:42
Cleveland	2:35	3:05	3:10	3:25	3:05	3:42
Duchy of Cornwall	2:39	3:09	3:14	3:29	3:09	3:46

	Men				Women	
Harlow	2:36	3:06	3:11	3:26	3:06	3:43
Huddersfield	2:35	3:05	3:10	3:25	3:05	3:42
Isle of Man	2:35	3:05	3:10	3:25	—	—
Isle of Wight	2:39	3:09	3:14	3:29	3:09	3:46
London ('81)	2:35	3:05	3:10	3:25	3:05	3:40
Milton Keynes	2:36	3:06	3:10	3:25	3:06	3:41
Newcastle	2:37	3:07	3:12	3:27	3:07	3:44
Newport	2:35	3:05	3:10	3:25	3:05	3:42
North Tyneside	2:35	3:05	3:10	3:25	3:05	3:42
Polytechnic	2:36	3:06	3:11	3:26	3:06	3:41
Preston-Morecambe	2:35	3:05	3:10	3:25	3:05	3:40
Rotherham	2:36	3:06	3:11	3:26	3:06	3:42
Sandbach	2:35	3:05	3:10	3:25	3:05	3:40
Scottish	2:35	3:05	3:10	3:25	—	—

Note that the Isle of Man and Scottish marathons are for men only, and that, although we have listed the RRC standard for men at Cambridge to give an idea of the course's difficulty, only men over 40 may enter.

You will notice an increasing number of marathons which are not yet categorised by the RRC. The boom has simply overwhelmed the club's resources. Secretary Peter Goodsell reckons that a dozen marathons in Britain are traditional annual fixtures but that in 1981 there were 40. 'Once marathons were a small part of the calendar; now everybody wants to organise one,' he says.

No marathon goes into the RRC standards scheme until it has been measured by their tough standards. The 1981 London course was accepted for length but no standards claims were accepted for it because the RRC were unhappy with the recording at the finish. There were too many discrepancies in the computer list.

Goodsell admits to being 'old fashioned' about road running. 'We should be interested in keeping standards up and not getting every Tom, Dick and Harry including disc jockeys in gold lamé suits doing it. The fun runs aren't road running as I know it.' But the club will get around gradually to measuring those of the new events which survive long enough, and perhaps even to learning to welcome them.

It is reckoned that in 1982 there will be as many as 70 marathons in the United Kingdom, and more than 300 in the United States. Almost every major Western city now has its marathon, and you can now find people's marathons in every continent.

Running Around The World

This is a list of some of the marathons you may care to try. It is not comprehensive but representative. Most are open to runners of all standards although some are limited by size. Precise dates change slightly each year but we have listed each in the month it has previously been held. Races are in England unless otherwise stated. Addresses are for entries.

JANUARY

Israel:

Sea of Galilee. Sports Federation, POB 4575, 4 Marmorek, Tel Aviv, Israel. Circles the Lake, all below sea level. Some years held before Christmas.

Bermuda:

PO Box 397, Devonshire, Bermuda, or any Bermuda Dept., of Tourism. Centred on National Stadium, Hamilton.

Miami:

Orange Bowl, Florida International University, Tamiani Trail, Miami 3319. Course flat but weather invariably hot.

FEBRUARY

New Orleans:

Mardi Gras Marathon, Box 2232, New Orleans, Louisiana 70176, USA. Point-to-point, 24 miles of it down the Lake Pontchartrain Causeway. Prevailing wind on your back.

Auckland:

City Marathon, Total Sport, Box 37-002, Parnell, Auckland, New Zealand. Round city race larger even than New York.

MARCH

Essonne (SW Paris):

Claude Noury, 3 Rue Corvisart, 91200, Athis-Mons, France. Undulating. Time limit 4½ hours.

Rome:

City Marathon, FIAL, 2 Via Franchetti, 00196, Rome, Italy. New in 1982.

Cornwall:

Duchy Marathon. W.A. Dobson, Barton Farm, Blackwater, Truro, Cornwall. Hilly point-to-point course, rated as tough even by elite. Runs from Land's End to Redruth.

APRIL

Boston:

Bill Cloney, PO Box 223, Boston, Massachusetts 02199, USA. Point-to-point, Hopkinton's Hayden Rowe Street to Prudential Centre, Boston. Largely downhill but has famous Heartbreak Hill (actually four hills) between 16 and 21 miles. Now limits entries, 2 hours 50min for men and 3 hours 10min for women. Lesser limits for the over-40s.

MAY

Vancouver:

Don Basham, 1200 Hornby St., Vancouver, British Columbia, V62 2E2, Canada. Circuit course from Robson Square. Starts at 7.30am.

Madrid:

Maratona Popular de Madrid, Salitre 43, Madrid 12, Spain. Round-the-city fun run.

London:

Recreation Dept., County Hall, London SE1. Totally flat, on scenic route from Greenwich along Thames to finish. Entries limited by numbers and close previous November.

Isle of Wight:

John Symonds, 31 Oakfield High Street, Ryde, IOW, PO33 IEJ. Circuit from Ryde Esplanade. Extremely tough and hilly.

Birmingham:

People's Marathon. John Walker, 111 Cooks Lane, Kingshurst, Birmingham B37 6NU. Two lap course in Chelmsley Wood, one hill on each lap. Limited to 4000 and excludes those who have bettered 2 hours 28min in previous 16 months.

Frankfurt:

Marathon Organisationsburo, D-6230 Frankfurt am Main 80, Postfach 80 06 45, Germany. River-side course, flat and traffic-free.

Paris:

Marathon de Paris, 23 Rue de la Sourdiere, 75001, Paris, France. Place du Trocadero to Eiffel Tower. Cobbles and heavy traffic. Time limit is 4½ hours.

JUNE

Sandbach:

John Nolan, 7 Kendal Place, Clayton, Newcastle, Staffs ST5 3QT. Fast, flat three-lap course.

Windsor:

Polytechnic Harriers Marathon, Jack Micklewright, 75 Sutton Rd., Heston, Hounslow, Middlesex TW5 0PN. One lap, starting at Windsor Castle and finishing one mile away at local stadium. Time limit 3 hours 20min.

JULY

Sandwell:

Mick Lockwood, Haden Hill Leisure Centre, Cradley Heath, Warley, W. Midlands. Flat and fast course with two slight inclines, starting and finishing at Dartmouth Park.

Milton Keynes:

International Marathon, 83 Fishponds Road, Tooting, London SW17 7LJ. Undulating on traffic free cycle paths. Time limit of 3 hours 45min.

Enschede:

International Foundation Marathon, Dahliastraat 154, 7531, DS Enschede, Holland. Biennial. Out-and-back flat course from Diekman Stadium. Time limit in 1981 3 hours 45min.

San Francisco:
Scott Thomason, PO Box 28385, San Francisco, Calif 94127, USA. Out-and-back course from Golden Gate Stadium with some hills. 7am start.

Helsinki:
City Marathon, c/o Finnish Athletics Federation, Suom Urheiluliitto, Box 25202, 00250, Helsinki 25, Finland.

AUGUST

Stockholm:
Box 100-23, S100 55, Stockholm, Sweden. Flat two-lap course through city centre, finishing at Olympic Stadium.

Newport:
9 Wyebank Close, Tutshill, Chepstow, Gwent. Four out-and-back laps.

Bolton:
Greater Manchester. Vince Regan, 424 St. Helens Rd., Bolton, Lancs. Through streets on circuit of Manchester suburbs. Undulating but aptly-named Plodder Lane is a tough hill at 24 miles. No entry or time limits.

Letterkenny:
Ulster Open, 7 College Row, Letterkenny, Co. Donegal. Eire. 2½ lap course following a river. Flat.

SEPTEMBER

Aberdeen:
Mel Edwards, 7 Middleton Terrace, Bridge of Don, Aberdeen, Scotland. Fast, city centre course.

Canvey Island:
CIAC Marathon, 49 Lottem Road, Canvey Island, Essex. Mostly at or below sea level, rising no more than two feet from start to finish.

Torbay:
David Thomas, Herald-Express, Harmsworth House, Barton Hill Road, Torquay. Paignton sea front start and finish, routing through Torquay and Newton Abbott.

Berlin West:
Sport-club Charlottenburg, Postfach 19 18 66, D-1000 Berlin 19, Germany. Reichstag start, Kurfestemdamm finish.

Eugene:
Nike-OTC, POB 10412, Oregon 97440, USA. Limited to 1,000; the elite are invited. Largely along flat highway.

Montreal:
Serge Arsenault, Montreal International, PO Box 1570, Montreal, Canada H3B 3L2. Flat, and it starts on bridge crossing St. Lawrence Seaway. Expects to finish in Olympic stadium from 1982.

OCTOBER

Cleveland:
County Leisure Services, PO Box 41, Middlesbrough. Three flattish laps around Middlesbrough.

Gloucester:
People's Marathon, Arthur Daley, 39 Mandevill Close, Gloucester. Flat around closed roads in city centre.

Stone:
Flying Fox, The Radfords, Stone, Staffordshire. For veterans only and including British Veterans championship.

New York:
NYRRC Marathon Entries, PO Box 1388 GPO, New York, NY10001, USA. Entries open June 2 and applications for forms must include 4½×9½inch self-addressed envelope and international reply coupon; better to join one of many entry-included travel agency packages if coming from Europe. Course tours five NY boroughs and is flat with a few inclines to bridges. No qualifying standard but heavily over-subscribed.

Athens:
Open International, GIFAS, 10 Panepistimou St. Athens 134, Greece. Starts from Tomb of Marathon, finishes Olympic Stadium. Tough, uphill course in a hot climate.

NOVEMBER

Barnsley:
Peter Gledhill, 9 Richard Road, Darton, Barnsley, S. Yorkshire. Undulating with some steep hills.

DECEMBER

Honolulu:

Honolulu Marathon Association, PO Box 27244, Chinatown Station, Honolulu, Hawaii, 96827. Mostly flat. Begins at 6am because of daytime heat.

On both sides of the Atlantic there are now travel agents organising trips to overseas marathons. Honolulu is a favourite from the States and Bermuda and Miami's Orange Bowl have both been included in agent's packages from Europe. New York and Boston, of course, are old standards for the travel trade.

This selection is only intended to give you a taste of the variety there is on offer once you are over the first hurdle and looking for a little more spice. In the directory at the back of the book there is a far more complete list of British marathons. Nobody could possibly want more in a single year!

CHAPTER 7

Race Day

THIS IS IT: the big day. The butterflies in the stomach are an inevitable and indeed, an essential part of the pre-race build-up so that when the gun goes, the running comes as a release. Wanting to get out there and get on with it is the sign of the juiced-up marathoner who's ready to do battle.

The sort of butterflies you *don't* want are those that come from either being under-trained or ill-prepared in some other way. You have to be honest with yourself about training. Only you know if you've put the work in and haven't cut too many corners. If you aren't honest with yourself, the challenge might be too much. Instead of being enriching, the race could be damaging, both physically and psychologically. Of course, some apprehension and self-doubt immediately before the race (especially if it's your first) is understandable; but if your approach to the marathon is marred by permanent lingering doubts about your ability to finish, rather than a sense of relish about the adventure to come, you should sit down and review your training diary and make a rational decision one way or the other. There will always be another race.

But the purpose of this chapter is not to dissuade you from reaching the starting line. Rather, it is to ensure that you arrive there free of unnecessary worries and feeling ready to go. In other words, to provide a plan of campaign which should help you avoid last-minute panics about silly details. With a little bit of forward planning you should be able to put yourself on 'automatic pilot' saving your energies for the real task in hand.

The Week Before

Training

As described in Chapter 4, training tapers off significantly during the build-up to the race. Some people prefer to rest up for the last two or three days before the race; I prefer one day off (either Race Day minus one or Race Day minus two) with easy jogging and a few strides on the other days. When you do run, the emphasis should be on suppleness and rhythm and you should be thinking positive thoughts. After all, the hard work's behind you and the pleasure is about to begin.

Unless you have to travel far, it can be a good idea to run over a section of the course — say the start or finish. In addition to this, a drive around the full course will not go amiss, just to familiarise yourself with the lie of the land.

Rest And Mental Preparation

Physiologically, you need plenty of rest and your training should no longer be putting you into 'overload'. It's not much fun starting a marathon with muscles still sore from a previous session.

So your training in this period is designed just to keep you ticking over and your other activities should be organised so as to leave plenty of time for sleep. Avoid being on your feet too much in the 48 hours before the race and try to ensure two really sound nights' sleep preceding the race. (Many athletes, used to travelling the day before a race or to being restless in bed the night before, insist it's the penultimate night's sleep that really matters and I've often found this to be the case.)

If you're worried about the possibility of nerves and excitement keeping you awake the night before Race Day, you might find it better to go to bed slightly later than usual and to try to tire yourself by going out to see a film for example. And it's not a bad idea, contrary to common belief, to have a beer as part of the relaxing and tiring process — assuming, of course, that you're not the type who gets hungover on half a pint of shandy.

Some of the larger marathons have a whole series of events surrounding them, including pasta parties on the eve of the race. You will not want to miss the atmosphere at such events and I'm not one to pass up free nosh and beer at any time, but it is salutary to note that you never see the top stars at such events. If it's easy to get to, you'll probably enjoy putting in appearance, but make sure you don't spend all night in a festive mood only to find you've got aching feet from standing up for too long.

For the rest of the time, pamper yourself as much as possible, even to the point of taking a day off work, if that's feasible. Go for

A mass start: the Gillette London Marathon, 1981

a short walk if the weather's nice or take yourself off to a play, concert or film. The point behind all this is that you want to feel good about being in the race and about preparing for it. That and the reduced training should, in theory, make you hungry for the race, like a dog under leash before the hare is sighted.

After all, it's not every day you run a marathon.

Diet

The general subject of eating to keep your body in shape to meet the demands of marathon training has been dealt with in Chapter 5. Ideally, all that needs to be added to that is the observation that the week before taking part in a marathon is not the time to start experimentation of any sort. So stick to what you know suits you and to what you enjoy.

But wherever two or three marathon runners are gathered together, there's sure to be talk of 'the diet'. For the unitiated, this means the carbohydrate loading diet which was first devised by a group of Swedish scientists working with long distance racing cyclists and attempting to build up their stores of muscle glycogen, the fuel which keeps the human body moving over a long period.

The possible benefits of the diet were spotted by Martin Hyman, a British international, who passed the word on to Ron Hill, a chemist and Britain's most experienced marathon runner. He tried it, refined it and had great success with it.

The carbohydrate loading diet involves the increasing of the glycogen store in the body. Glycogen is your chief source of fuel in long distance running. It is a carbohydrate stored as a sugar in the muscles, but after 18 or more miles of continuous running, it virtually dries up. The tiredness, weakness and absolute lethargy that can hit you at this stage of the race has come to be known as 'The Wall'. The body then has to switch to other fuel (chiefly body fat) and will do this with varying degrees of success depending on how fit you are.

Burning fat, however, is not as efficient as burning glycogen. The scientists therefore sought a way of increasing this glycogen store by dietary manipulation. The classic and most severe form of the diet (known either as the 'bleed-out' or 'carbo-loading' diet) as adapted for marathon running consists roughly of the following diet programme.

Time markers waiting to be positioned at the start of the New York City Marathon

The finishing funnels awaiting the hordes at the end of the first London Marathon

Seven days before the race, you run 20 miles to deplete your glycogen. Then, for the next three days you stay off all carbohydrates, during which time the body is tricked into creating glycogen of its own to fill the gap. From lunchtime three days before the long run, you switch to a diet *very high* in carbohydrates — pasta, potatoes, cakes, sweet sticky things, the whole works! — until Race Day. Theoretically you can double the normal glycogen content of muscles in this way. But there are major drawbacks:

1. The 20 miler so close to the race is not a good idea for most runners.
2. The light training you do for the rest of the week will probably be unpleasant due to the carbo-starving.
3. You put on weight and may arrive at the starting line unduly heavy and feeling lethargic.
4. You may feel rotten for the whole time — despite the licence to binge on life's goodies just before the race. Sleep can be affected and it's possible you lower your resistance to infection during this period. Some people find the benefits late in the race spectacular, others have taken only a few extra seconds off their time and even more just feel too bad and abandon the diet halfway.
5. The long term effects of repeated use of the diet are not known and in any case, the body appears to get used to the trickery and adapts less well on successive occasions.

How do you know if you should try the diet? The answer is — it's interesting to know about it, but *don't* try it. The main reason is, it only really works for the top runners, already at the peak of their fitness. This is the icing on their cake, if you like. It is not even clear whether a slower runner, going at his training pace, will actually deplete the glycogen supplies on a bleed-out run. On top of that, your body has enough to cope with on your first marathon without being shocked by a radical new diet.

You should only start to consider using the diet when you are an experienced runner and have tried it out in a non-competitive situation to see how you react. Wait till you're up with the élite, in other words when you've exhausted all the other methods (like running more miles, for example!).

In the meantime, however, there's no harm in plundering the theory for a few ideas. It may well be of help to simply adopt the modified loading-up procedure in the final days before the race to top up your carbohydrate stores, making the evening meal the night before the race the last heavy one.

I personally feel ambivalent about such bodily manipulation – and so does Dr David Costill, running's most famous physiologist. He discovered that drinking two cups of unsweetened black coffee about an hour before the race can improve performance because the caffeine acts on blood fats to make them more readily usable as fuel before calling on the glycogen stores. But he tries to play this down, noting that caffeine is, of course, a drug. And the use of that word, in particular, makes me think. (Once again, if you do want to try this, don't make Race Day the first time: as always, do a dry run first.)

Do not be tempted to carry on 'loading up' on Race Day with sweet things. Eating sugar or glucose does raise your blood sugar levels (a good thing initially) but it also produces an 'insulin reaction' which causes blood sugar levels to drop rapidly thereafter. So lay off the glucose tablets and the sticky buns on race day.

Race Logistics

This includes everything from making sure you have not forgotten your shoes, to checking on journey time and where and when to check in.

About a week before the race, sit down with all the details you've been sent by the organisers and go through them carefully. Then make a timetable of things you have to do by a certain time on the day. If you haven't already been sent a number, study the registration details carefully, noting that the very big races (London, New York etc) have registration and number collection in the three or four days before the race and not at all on Race Day itself. Familiarity with the procedure will mean there are no last-minute flaps. Always allow more time than you think is necessary and aim to be early: several hundred runners queueing for numbers and pins half an hour before the start is not a pretty sight.

Then, make your transport plans. If the marathon is more than about an hour's drive away or if it's an early morning start and you have to use public transport it will be worthwhile considering staying overnight close to the race HQ. Organisers often offer cut-price accommodation at local hotels, but ask about this well in advance.

The next thing to commit to paper is your kit list, which should look something like this:

Marathoner's Race Day Kit

To wear	**To use**
Running shoes	Toilet tissues
Socks	Vaseline/skin cream
Shorts	Plasters
Pants	Liniment/rub
Vest	General first aid kit
T-shirt or warm-up top	Foot/talcum powder
Track suit	Towel } if changing there
Spare top } disposable	Soap } if changing there
Spare bottoms } disposable	
Large plastic bag (bin-liner)	**Paperwork:**
Headband/wristband	Pace chart
if worn	Race instructions
Rain suit	Map
Hat	Number (if supplied)
Gloves	Safety pins

Make sure you have this all collected together a couple of days before Race Day so that you aren't fiddling with shoe laces the night before the race when you should be relaxing. This will also remind you if your favourite pair of shorts is still in your bag caked in mud from last Sunday's training run!

Although you want to feel good and look the part on Race Day, don't treat it as a 'Sunday best' occasion by saving up new kit or — worse still — new shoes for the race: everything you wear must be tried and tested. Shoes especially can cause problems for the debutant marathoner. It is natural to want to use a pair of racers with that unique go-faster ingredient the manufacturers have kindly built in to them, but unless you're used to running in lightweight shoes (i.e. you've done several long training sessions in them with no ill effects) I recommend that you stick to your favourite trainers. They may weigh a few ounces more, but they know you and you know them and comfort rather than speed is going to be the order of the day initially.

One final point on shoes: don't be *too* loyal to a particular pair, however fond you've grown of them. About a month before the race, check the ones you plan to race in carefully for signs of wear. If you're starting to burst out the uppers or the wear on the sole is starting to make them lop-sided, now is the time to act. Either get them resoled (consult your sports shop) or buy a new pair and start breaking them in.

Race Day

If you've followed the checklists above, Race Day should be relatively relaxed. All you need to do is have a small meal, get changed and get yourself to the start.

What To Eat

There are some people who swear by waking up and getting straight on with the race, skipping breakfast on the way. That may work for them, but unless you've proved to yourself in dry runs before that it really does suit you, this course of action does not make good nutritional sense. You have a long day ahead of you, including strenuous physical exercise and the body needs regular nourishment.

Most races are now run in the morning. For a start time of, say, 10.30am, I recommend a light breakfast at not later than 8am. Choose easily digestible foods and things you are used to. Cereal, toast, scrambled or boiled eggs, honey, and jam are all — in suitable permutations — standard favourites for the pre-race breakfast, accompanied by as much liquid (orange juice, tea, coffee or whatever) as you like.

Not recommended are fried foods or large portions of meat which tend to take a long time to digest. Similarly, steer clear of items like tomatoes whose skins are not readily digestible. In general, commonsense and personal taste will dictate the sort of meal you have: the principle to bear in mind is that you want to take on board a bit of last-minute fuel, but not to have a full stomach when you start running.

After the meal and before leaving for the race, empty your bowels. Unless the nervous excitement really gets to you, this should mean you don't have to join a straggling queue for toilets at the start or in the changing rooms, though some runners prefer to go one last time as close to the start as possible.

As long as you don't feel bloated as a result, drinking before the start is a good idea and very necessary if the weather is hot. Physiologists recommend that half a pint of water taken *not more* than half an hour before the start will ensure you are topped up. What you are seeking to do is ensure that the liquid is where you need it. — absorbed into the blood stream. Research in the Physiology Department at Guy's Hospital Medical School in London shows that one of the factors affecting the rate of absorption is the rate of emptying of the stomach and that slightly salted water (a 0.6 per cent solution or half a teaspoon of salt to a pint of water) leaves the stomach faster than plain H_2O.

Generally, the Western diet is, if anything, too salty so extra salt is not normally required as a matter of routine even for those in hard training, but this is a specific instance where salt has a particular role to play. Some people may not like the salty taste: try it before a training run to see how you react.

As an alternative, you may wish to use one of the commercial drinks such as Staminade, Gatorade or XL-1. These are electrolyte replacement drinks (electrolytes are the salts or irons — sodium, potassium, chloride, magnesium etc which regulate the amount of water in your cells and which help generate the electrical impulses telling the muscles to contract and move) designed to replace the salts you lose in sweat.

Again, if you plan to use them on Race Day, experiment with the various drinks on the market before and, especially if you intend to drink such preparations on the run. What the stomach accepts in ordinary circumstances, it may actively dislike during exercise. So go for a long run first having drunk some before, then call in at home for more midway and carry on running to see how you feel.

Drinking During The Race

In the really big, mass marathons, there is usually not the facility to provide personal drinks. Instead the organisers will make available perhaps one electrolyte drink, a dilute fruit juice and plain water at the feeding stations. Remember that water is the most important thing you need on the run; added ingredients may be useful but the basic need is for fluid — and hardly anyone reacts badly to plain old water.

If, however, you are able to provide your own drinks, add this to your preparation list in the week before and when registering for the race, leave your drinks in small plastic screw-top bottles, clearly marked with your number in the appropriate place.

These should then be waiting for you at appointed drinks stations on the course. The IAAF and AAA rules specify that feeding stations shall be provided at three miles and at three mile intervals thereafter (in some events they are more frequent). You are strongly advised to make use of the stations even if you lose a few seconds each time. The rule in marathons, especially when hot, is *drink little but often*. You should not wait until you feel thirsty before starting drinking: once you've reached that point, the damage is done and you won't be able to 'top up' sufficiently to recover fully. Fluid imbalance can lead to excessive tiring, muscle cramping and mental disorientation. It is not pleasant, especially when there are still six miles to go.

Drinks are normally provided in plastic cups and if there are plenty of helpers, they will be handed to you at the roadside. Get yourself into a position at the side of the road to accept one — or, if necessary pick one up on the run from the table as you pass. If time is really important, you will not want to slow down, but in practice, that's the only way to make sure you don't spill most of the drink down your front. A natural slowing-up occurs at drink (or 'feeding' stations as they are also known) because of the congestion of bodies and the fact that the road will be covered in excess liquid and slippery plastic cups. So take care. To drink on the run, pour half the cup away and sip slowly from the rest, then toss the cup away and carry on.

Sponging stations are usually provided midway between feeding stations. In hot conditions, you'll find these essential; at other times, it's a matter of choice. (You can of course use water from your cup to bathe your face and, to return the compliment a sponge can become an impromptu drinking vessel — but unless you're in the lead this can be inadvisable: you'll probably be using a recycled sponge which has lain on the road and whose water is far from fresh!)

When you take a sponge, first squeeze from it the excess water. You may be longing for a cold shower, but running for miles in

Screw-top bottles containing personal drinks

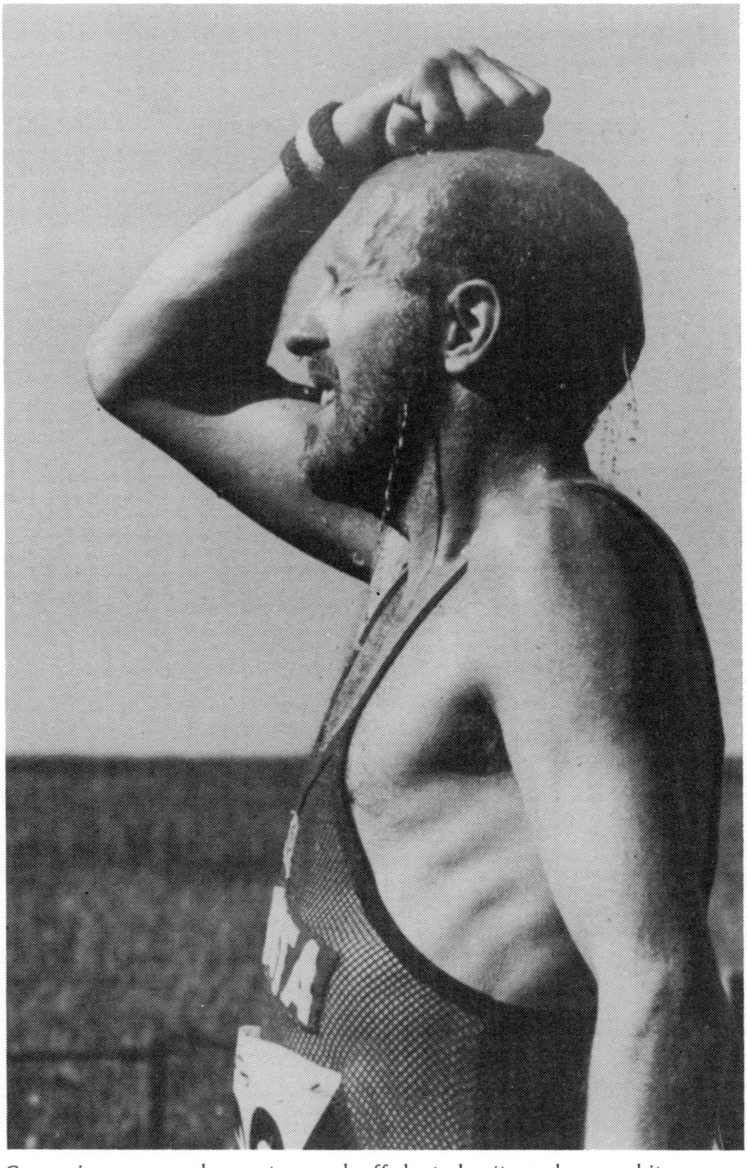

Sponging: a good way to cool off, but don't soak your kit in the process heavy wet kit is no fun and even the snuggest fitting shoes can become chafing, waterlogged torture chambers if you're too profligate with the water. Make the sponge merely damp and wipe your face and neck and perhaps squeeze gently into your hair. The main heat-generating part of your body is the muscle group in the thighs and many experienced runners find using the sponge on the inside of the thighs helps to delay the onset of muscle tightness and tiredness in that area.

The Hour Before The Race

We have, however, run a bit ahead of ourselves discussing pre- and mid-race replenishment. We must back up a little and check the routine immediately before the race. An hour before the off, everything should be done. You should be checked-in and registered and know where you need to report and when. To avoid the crush in the changing rooms, I prefer to be changed, too, by this time, although some people use changing as a time-filler. It depends on the size and quality of the changing facilities, but fighting for space in a seething mass of people is not the ideal preparation for a marathon. Many races, of course, do not provide changing accomodation, but even when they do I nearly always arrive changed from home or hotel, just in case. This will be the time for a final visit to the toilet if necessary — and with thousands of others thinking the same thing and feeling the same pressure, this can be more time-consuming than you think!

When changing, remember to tape and/or grease up. This is a time-honoured tradition for marathon runners, recognising the fact that during two or more hours of continuous running, constant rubbing of clothing against certain parts of the body can become painful even blood-drawing chafing. Some people put sticking plaster over exposed points such as nipples (men and women!), others prefer a liberal coating of Vaseline. I use a nappy cream on all relevant parts: armpits, nipples, crotch and the top of the thigh where the hem of your shorts might rub.

It can also be advisable to powder your feet and socks to try to keep them cooler and reduce friction. Or again, use Vaseline all over, especially around the toes.

Finally, of greater psychological help, perhaps, is a general rub-down. All of this activity is pleasantly warming and if you can get somebody to give you a quick massage so much the better. I like to head off to the start with muscles pleasantly tingling from an application of a 'Deep Heat'-type liniment.

It's useful to have somebody with you just before the race — a kind of second who takes the strain for you, the performer. They might drive you there, pick up your number if necessary and check out the arrangements generally. They can also keep you occupied in the tedious waiting time unless you prefer the solitary approach (in which case, go away and lie down somewhere warm and quiet).

You will probably want to jog a little, maybe do a few strides just to remind yourself you haven't forgotten how to do it, but a final warm-up, apart from a few of your loosening exercises is not necessary. Save that for the gentle first mile when you're feeling your way into the race — and always allow for a couple of minutes extra for that on your pace plan (see below) because of the early crush

Agree with your 'second' what is happening to your kit and where you will meet up with him/her at the end. Organisers usually provide plastic bags with numbered tags for your tracksuit to be left in one central point and some also designate meeting places at the finish, complete with signs indicating the first letter of your name.

If the race is computerised, you may need to go through a 'bar code' check as you make your way to the start. Once through that, there's no turning back! You may have had to deposit your track suit already but there will still be some waiting. So, if the weather is unpleasant, use your spare kit — an old, discardable sweat top and pants or a bin-liner.

Try to keep moving around, jogging gently on the spot. If it's really cold, make friends quickly and huddle together, sharing each other's warmth! Start looking for the time signs at the start: mass starts are characterised by time markers indicating where to stand for your estimated running time (these are usually in 15-minute time bands). It's in your interest to make an honest assessment of your performance: joining the 2:30 crowd when you're really after 3:15 will force you to start faster than is good for you and will mean you're getting in the way of others.

You can either dispense with your spare, discardable warm-up kit immediately before the start (away from the course itself) or shed it en route — but be considerate about other runners and spectators.

Pacing Yourself

Only you know what is realistic to expect from your training performances. There is something to be said for going into your first marathon with no pre-conceived notions of time and just enjoying yourself, but most people will have a target. Many people wear a digital watch (press it when you cross the starting line rather than at the gun if you're back in the ranks of a big field) and there are often timed points along the course (usually at five mile intervals and halfway). This will allow you to compute your mile times and see what time you're on target for (see the Pace Chart). If you know what you're looking for, you can write down the requisite mile of five-mile 'split times' on the back of your number or on a piece of paper attached to your vest. Some people write on their palms or arms, but I found this had disappeared at the first sponging station when I did it.

The best advice on pace in general is — make it even. A steady rhythm is far better than a series of enthusiastic but tiring bursts through the field. Especially when the going gets tough, it can be useful to have a partner running with you as long as your ability is roughly equal. You may have to make a decision later in the race about splitting up, but keeping each other company and in check in the early miles is useful. If you're alone, you'll find a marathon field very friendly and unless you're deadly serious about this particular mission, teaming up with a group and joining in sporadic conversation can actually help, rather than hinder, your concentration. Certainly, the miles seem to slip by faster.

We have referred earlier to 'The Wall' and ways of trying to avoid it or mitigate its effects in advance. All you can do now really is hope . . . and drink. It's often said that the 20 mile mark in a marathon is the halfway point but there's no need to build up an irrational fear about the last few miles. Just take them as they come and tell yourself that slowly, but surely, you're pulling towards the finish, a long rest and a unique sense of achievement.

Pace Chart*

1 MILE	5 MILES	10 MILES	15 MILES	20 MILES	MARATHON
4:50	24:10	48:20	1:12:30	1:36:40	2:06:44
5:00	25:00	50:00	1:15:00	1:40:00	2:11:06
5:10	25:50	51:40	1:17:30	1:43:20	2:15:28
5:20	26:40	53:20	1:20:00	1:46:40	2:19:50
5:30	27:30	55:00	1:22:30	1:50:00	2:24:12
5:40	28:20	56:40	1:25:00	1:53:20	2:28:34
5:50	29:10	58:20	1:27:30	1:56:40	2:32:57
6:00	30:00	1:00:00	1:30:00	2:00:00	2:37:19
6:10	30:50	1:01:40	1:32:30	2:03:20	2:41:41
6:20	31:40	1:03:20	1:35:00	2:06:40	2:46:03
6:30	32:30	1:05:00	1:37:30	2:10:00	2:50:25
6:40	33:20	1:06:40	1:40:00	2:13:20	2:54:47
6:50	34:10	1:08:20	1:42:30	2:16:40	2:59:10
7:00	35:00	1:10:00	1:45:00	2:20:00	3:03:32
8:00	40:00	1:20:00	2:00:00	2:40:00	3:29:45
9:00	45:00	1:30:00	2:15:00	3:00:00	3:55:58
10:00	50:00	1:40:00	2:30:00	3:20:00	4:22:11
11:00	55:00	1:50:00	2:45:00	3:40:00	4:48:24
12:00	60:00	2:00:00	3:00:00	4:00:00	5:14:38
13:00	1:05:00	2:10:00	3:15:00	4:20:00	5:40:51
14:00	1:10:00	2:20:00	3:30:00	4:40:00	6:07:04
15:00	1:15:00	2:30:00	3:45:00	5:00:00	6:33:17

The Finish

You will probably be met by queues of people all over the road and will be directed into one by an official. This is the funnel system where individual funnels are filled up in strict order. Don't panic if people finishing behind you are led ahead of you in an adjacent funnel: they will be counted in after you.

As soon as you stop, check the digital clock, if there is one, or your own watch for your time. Even with sophisticated computer technology, the official results often have a margin of error of up to 20 seconds, and don't of course, take into account the time you spent reaching the starting line!

Part or all of your number may be removed as you leave the funnel and you may also be given your medal here (if there is one). Once out of the finish, follow directions for clothing and take a blanket if offered to avoid rapid cooling. Get into your track suit as soon as possible and *try to keep moving*, however slowly. After 26 and a bit miles, this may seem rather perverse, but it not only keeps you warm, it also helps to prevent the worst of post-marathon stiffness

*Courtesy of *Running* magazine.

The elation of completing the magic distance — topped off by a medal

The finish: keep warm and take some liquid as soon as possible.

by keeping the blood circulating and preventing the pooling of waste products in the muscles.

If you are feeling bad, medical help should be on hand. Most people simply need a sit-down and a warm blanket and a few minutes' rest. Unless it's a roasting day, it's not a good idea simply to flop on the floor and lie there.

At this point a knowledge of the finish facilities and their layout comes into its own, as does a set plan to meet up with friends or relations at an agreed point. Look out also for refreshments: it is important to keep drinking as much fluid as possible for several hours after the marathon. A simple guide is that if your urine is straw-coloured, you are still dehydrated. Keep drinking until it returns to its usual, paler colour.

CHAPTER 8

Marathon Profiles

Alberto Salazar

Running down Fourth Avenue, just before 67th Street, Alberto Salazar knew there was no way out. The weather was perfect, 50°F and overcast and the wind nothing to complain about. 'Well, I thought, you had to open your big mouth, so now you're going to have to deliver.'

What Salazar knew he had to deliver on the 25th of October, 1981 in the streets of New York City was the fastest time ever run for the marathon, better than the 2:09:01 run by Holland's Gerard Nijboer in 1980 and better even than the 2:08:34 run by Australian Derek Clayton in 1969 which Americans have always suspected was achieved on a short course.

It was more than should have been expected of any man running in only his second marathon, even one who had won the New York classic in his first marathon in 2:09:41, the fastest first-time marathon ever run. But Salazar was not just any man. He had boldly, some said rashly, given his predicted time on his entry form as 2:08.

In the normal course of events it would have been dismissed as an attempt to psyche out the opposition. But Salazar had form as a tipster, and nobody knew this particular horse better than its owner. The previous year he had predicted a time of 2:10 for himself and nobody was going to argue with an error factor of a quarter of one per cent, 19 seconds in 2 hours 10 min. That's as good as tipping a rank outsider to win the Derby by a nose, and see it do it by a head.

To beat Clayton's time, he had to average 4 minutes 54 seconds for every mile, and only a handful of men had run the distance at even five minute mile pace. To ask a rookie marathoner who had never run a single sub-four minute mile in his life to do it was barely reasonable.

Yet those in the Salazar camp were betting on it. Rich Phaigh, his masseur at his club, Athletics West in Eugene, Oregon, was taking $100 bets on it. He knew that Salazar's interval miles on Eugene's wood-chip trail were 12 seconds faster than in 1980. He knew that he had 17 weeks of uninterupted training. Athletics is not an exact art, let alone a science, but the conditioners are not to be deceived.

Making predictions naturally increases pressure and that is an extra dimension that is never part of the equation of physical fitness. Salazar had not meant to boast of a 2:08 time but born-again Christians such as he do not make a habit of deceit. 'If someone asks me a question I simply try to answer truthfully,' he said.

One by one Salazar's predictions kept coming true. Ten miles passed as he had said it would in 49:04, thanks largely to Irishman Louis Kenny who was running like a fox before hounds, clicking off sub-five minute miles that would have taken him to a world best had he lasted. Kenny did not but Salazar went all the way, 1:04:10 at half way, a 17th mile in a breathtaking 4 minutes 37 seconds, an 18th in 4:42 and the 19th in 4:49.

When he hit 20 miles in 1:37:29 after saying he wanted to be there in 1:38, even he knew that the record was his. 'I knew I could run the rest of the course in half an hour. All I had to do was maintain the pace, I didn't have to pick it up.' He finished in 2:08:13. The record was no longer in doubt.

So it happened that for only the second time in more than half a century an American came to run the fastest marathon ever; an American whose prime ambitions lay on the track and whose running style, in the words of *New York Times* correspondent Neil Amdur, 'must warm the hearts of neighbourhood joggers who fret about being laughed at'.

Salazar was born in Havana, Cuba in 1958, the son of a friend of Fidel Castro and a supporter of the revolution. When his father fled the island, disillusioned with Communism, he was just two years old. The family moved first to Florida then to Manchester, Conn., and finally to Wayland, Mass. By Sixth grade Salazar was known across New England for his running and by his senior year in high school there were only three 'prep' runners in the entire country who could compete with him.

He was at high school when he had two 5000 metre wins over the Russians in the USSR-USA junior matches and at 17 he was placed 24th in the American AAU senior national cross country championship. He also made the American team for the world junior cross country championship, finishing fifth individually in a winning American team.

After school, he chose faraway Eugene and the University of Oregon because of the reputation of its track team and coach Bill Dellinger, the 1964 Olympic 5000 metres bronze medallist, disappointing many establishments closer to his home. But the impact he made in Oregon, the *de facto* running capital of the country, was hardly sensational. He failed to finish in the NCAA cross country championships as a freshman and was only ninth a year later.

Salazar had strength but he lacked speed. After he had done all the work in a race his rivals knew they would invariably out-kick him. In the 1979 NCAA 10,000 metres, the Tanzanian Suleiman Nyambui, running for El Paso let him lead for 20 laps, and 230 metres from home burned him off into third place.

'All these kickers who are afraid to take the lead and work in a race are just a bunch of chickens,' said Salazar with feeling, but it was the reaction of one who knew he was playing into the opposition's hands. With him pace-making out front, they could not help but see his achilles heel.

It was revealed to all on national television on ABC's 20/20 programme where running-scientist Dr David Costill, of Ball State University, examined him. A muscle biopsy by the exercise physiologist who wrote the renowned book *A Scientific Approach To Distance Running* revealed that Salazar possessed 92 per cent slow-twitch fibres. Put simply, it proved Salazar was no sprinter!

However he has immense courage, a quality which few athletes possess. He is so tough with himself that Dellinger has often been forced to put a restraining influence on his work-outs. Often he is pushing 140 miles a week. 'With Al, it is not a question of whether he's done the work. It is trying to hold him back, keeping him from going too far,' says his coach.

Nothing proved too much for him if it might improve his performances. At the beginning of the 1980 Olympic year he took

Alberto Salazar

himself off to Kenya to live alone at high altitude for five months. He lasted only three weeks there, beaten by boredom, but he believed the theory held good. For weeks he ran around Eugene with an altitude-simulator, called a pO_2 exerciser, strapped like a diver's tanks to his back with a mask covering nose and mouth restricting his air supply and simulating an altitude of 8000 feet.

Sometimes he even pushed himself beyond his own limits. In the 1979 Falmouth 7 he ran himself so hard in temperatures of around 85°F that he collapsed. Rushed to the medical tent, his body temperature soared to 104°F and, fearing for his life, a priest was called to administer the Last Rites.

Everybody knew Salazar was good, but on the track in an international context that was not sufficient for him. He was not American national record holder, and it was obvious to everybody close to him that he was one of those runners best suited to greater distances.

It was like asking an aspiring Hamlet to play a Pantomime Dame, or in the context of Marty Liquori's dismissive description of 'track is Carnegie Hall; road racing is just rock 'n roll'. Salazar wanted to be a track great. 'Road races mean very little to me,' he said. 'I'd trade anything I've done for a world track record'.

Even so he could not postpone the inevitable for ever. 'Without a doubt I'm perfectly suited to be a marathoner. I can say that because of my running style and because of the high mileage I've always put in. I can run 2:10, 2:11 first time out. I just want to beat Billy Rodgers at his own game.'

Finally in October, 1980, he gave it a try, and as so many had suspected the Salazar shuffle was as devastating on the road as the Ali shuffle had been in the ring. And the predictions were just as accurate. He ran the New York in 2:09:41, and his Greater Boston Track Club team-mate Bill Rodgers, the American record holder was fifth. 'Under the right conditions I can run it faster,' he said.

His 1981 preparations began on June 8 after a disappointing showing in the NCAA 10,000 metres. He was not to take a day off running again until October 25, and for the last 12 weeks he averaged 106 miles a week, smashing the course record at the Falmouth 7 by 24 seconds and running a personal record of 27:40 for third place in the World Cup 10,000 metres.

He revealed a typical week of training before he ran in New York. Monday: morning, 10 miles at about 6 minute mile pace, usually on wood-chip trail; afternoon, 8 miles, including 8 × 10 metres in 30 seconds with 30 seconds rest; Nautilus training.

Tuesday: morning, 8 miles; afternoon, 3½ miles warm-up, 6 one mile work-outs averaging 4:30 with one-quarter mile jog and a rest in 2:30.

Wednesday: morning, 10 miles; afternoon, 8 miles.

Thursday: morning, 3 mile warm-up, 5 mile run on a dirt track in 23:57 (4:47.5 pace), 3½ mile cool down; afternoon, 6 miles.

Friday: morning, 10 miles; afternoon, 8 miles.

Saturday: morning, 4 mile warm-up, fast ¾ mile on track, 4 miles, fast ¾ mile, 4 miles, fast ¾ mile, 4 miles.

Sunday: one 20 mile run in 1:57:30. Weekly total = 128 miles.

He had made his prediction and was not going to be proven wrong. Salazar ran the fastest time the world has ever seen the marathon run, and then gave it another thought. 'You know, I think the potential is there to go two or three minutes faster. So a time of around 2:05 is possible.'

And who's to argue with Alberto Salazar?

Allison Roe

Women drivers must be taken seriously now that a French woman has won an international rally outright. Jokes about women marathoners are also wearing thin. Allison Roe has beaten Frank Shorter in a marathon.

Of course, it could never happen. Shorter, the Olympic champion in 1972 and runner-up in 1976, is a legend and Roe is a woman who had to walk to finish her first marathon. Yet the results are there, in the stark black-and-white official figures of the 1981 New York marathon. Roe, 113th in 2:25:29; Shorter, 117th in 2:25:45. The legend may need some re-writing.

There were still 112 men in front of the fastest woman marathoner the world has ever seen but for how much longer? Allison Roe had not run a marathon two years ago and she is still only 25. What might have happened had the previous women's record holder, Greta Waitz, not been forced out of the race by severe shin splints? And what will happen as Roe learns and gains more experience?

She is certainly learning fast. In less than two years she has progressed by more than 26 minutes and transformed herself from a track runner in search of an event to a queen of the road. And all by one of those curious twists of fate. It was the New Zealand summer of 1980-81. A road season injury had sidelined her, she had missed a lot of training and when her track season began badly, she looked around for a different challenge. The Choysa marathon happened to be held in February, and she entered. It never occured to her that she might finish. She had never run further in training than 18 miles, and then only once.

Her average weekly mileage was only between 30 and 40, and she told herself she would call it a day between 12 and 15 miles. She did try. In her own words, 'the crowd was so persuasive I just had to keep going and finish'. But she was reduced to walking at times, and her time of 2:51:45 suggested no more than competence at the distance.

But there was another twist. She was the first New Zealand woman to finish. The prize for that was a trip to America for the Nike/OTC marathon in Eugene, Oregon. 'Had the trip not been the prize, I'm sure that I wouldn't have ever run another marathon,' she said, recalling the pain she felt at Choysa. 'But I decided to train and really make a go of Oregon.'

She pushed her mileage to an average for 15 weeks of 68 miles a week, training every day and finding time from her secretarial job for three extra morning sessions. In Oregon she breezed it, third in 2:34:29, finishing feeling good and convinced she could run faster. So were the boys she ran with on the Waitakeres near her native Auckland.

But when she tried again in an all-women's race in Tokyo, still running around 68 miles weekly, she attempted more than a respectable time. She was trying to win, and she learned the difference the hard way. Just before 20 miles, she hit 'The Wall'.

'It was almost indescribable,' she recalled. 'I felt pressure around my shoulders and a dizzy disorientated feeling. Suddenly my stride rhythm and pattern — everything — went to pieces. I was a total wreck. I was forced to halt and jog and take all the orange juice I could on the side of the road. It was really horrific.' She finished fourth in 2:42:24, her feet badly blistered.

This could be put down to inexperience but she was learning. Two months later she won the Auckland International in her own backyard in 2:36:14, and in April 1981 took America by storm by winning the Boston, not only beating local heroine Patti Catalano but running the second fastest ever run by a woman, 2:26:46. That was her first New Zealand national record. Six months later in New York she set her first world record. Allison Roe was queen of the road.

As Allison Deed she had spent many years on the verge of something which had never quite materialised. When she became Mrs Roe, wife of American chiropracter Richard Roe, a few months after her first marathon, everything fell into place.

Allison Deed was a promising teenage tennis player in her native Auckland. Only at 17 did she start running, and that after winning high jump titles at high school. Within a year she was New Zealand's youngest ever senior cross country champion at the age of 18, and a member of their team which was runner-up in the world cross country championship in Morocco.

She was coached then by the former British distance runner Gordon Pirie but it was soon apparent that she suffered that vexing deficiency of so many runners — lack of speed. She became New Zealand champion at cross country and road races but her track times were not fast enough to class her internationally. And when the longest track race is 300 metres, where does a woman go?

The 1980s, of course, have brought the answer, and Allison Roe has found it. It has meant changes for her. 'It's been the turning point for me. I was very lazy, only running around 40 miles a week. Now I'm pushing 70. I know that is not so much by the standards of some Americans but my mileage is harder. To me consistency is the key, and for the first time in my life I'm training consistently.'

There have been technical corrections, too. Track runners run on their toes. With her long, relaxed stride off a height of 5ft 8½in, it was a style which suited her. But the marathon is about efficiency. 'I've had to concentrate on trying to lower myself, to run a little flatter. On your toes, running long distances, your calf muscles tighten very quickly.'

The old technique is seen now only downhill. There it re-appears naturally as the momentum throws her forward. A course like Boston suits her well. After all she cannot leave her Auckland home without going up or down hill. Most of her running is done on hills, and the rest on beaches and golf courses, natural surfaces with natural undulations.

The summer before the New York race, where she knew she would be meeting world record holder Waitz for the first time, Roe competed frequently in the States. It almost led to her missing New York.

Trouble first arose when she had run in the Cascade Run Off 15 kilometre in Oregon, the first event on the Association of Road Running Athletes' openly professional circuit. She and two other New Zealand women, Lorraine Moller and Anne Audain had been warned not to run it by the New Zealand Federation. They ignored the advice. 'It's a moral issue,' said Allison. 'The old system is corrupt.'

They took the first three places. Allison's prize was 4,000 dollars — and certain disqualification from all future amateur races. The other two women accepted disqualification but Allison succeeded in negotiating with the NZAAA to put the prize in trust with them. Until a week before the New York race she was still uncertain whether the American Federation and the International Amateur Athletic Federation would accept that compromise.

By the time they had, Allison was suffering from tendonitis in the right ankle. Only ultrasonic treatment two days before the big day kept her in the race.

In the end she ran the race almost perfectly. She was even-paced all the way, around 27:45 for each five miles and passing 20 miles in another world best of 1:50:32. The only pity was that Greta Waitz had not lasted the race.

The two had run together, Allison staying back with the Norwegian thinking she was the danger. But Waitz was in pain, her sore shins crippling her. 'Why don't you go ahead,' she told Roe at 22 kilometres. It was the last they saw of each other, and the last moment Waitz retained her hold on the record.

Can women now edge even closer to the men? Roe is clearly thinking that way. 'Women will have to start thinking a bit more like men, and training like them. They'll have to forget about worrying about their limitations. And you can only do that running against men.'

Toshihiko Seko

It is called by its creator *Zensoho*. In Japanese than means 'running with Zen'. In English, it translates as 'running with a clear mind'. In lay terms, it probably means no more than concentrating. It is certainly effective in anybody's language.

Toshihiko Seko practises *Zensoho*, and he has won the Fukuoka marathon three times and the Boston once in 1981. He reads and studies the scriptures, too, and the works of Buddhists and other philosophers. After a race at home, he will retire to the temple to meditate.

Seko is one of the world's great marathoners. He does not yet have the Japanese national record but then Shigeru Soh's time of 2:09:06 is the third fastest in history. What Seko has is the best win-ratio of any current runner, seven runs, four wins and one second, those five all in Fukuoka or Boston, the two most prestigious races for any marathoner.

Seko also has Kiyoshi Nakamura for a coach. It was he who taught Seko *Zensoho*, just as he has taught it to scores more of Japan's best runners. Nine of Japan's national records are held by the 90 current members of his private track club. Seko holds two more world records at 25 and 30 km.

How much *Zensoho* contributed to Seko beating Bill Rodgers at their last two meetings is incalculable. Certainly it has much to do with the extraordinary relationship which exists between runner and coach.

Nakamura does not just run his club. He owns it. He owns the runners in it, too, body and soul. As Seko says: 'I am what I am and who I am because of him. I believe in everything he says. Everything in me, down to the smallest detail, has changed since I met Nakamura sensei.'

Sensei means master. It is what all his runners call him. Once he used to beat them when they did not perform to his expectations. They called him Satan. Now he only scolds them. 'I discovered that words were more effective,' says Nakamura.

His coaching methods are dismissed by some as fanaticism. 'Worse than a religion,' wrote one journalist. 'Crazy' said another. But in a country accustomed to fanaticism, to the tradition of ultimate obedience in the Shogun, the philosophy is accepted unquestioningly. When Seko rejected Nakamura at first and returned home, his father locked him out, called Nakamura and told him. 'Do whatever you must with him; he's yours.'

Now Nakamura controls every minute of his day apart from the four hours daily he works for the S and B Shokuhin Co., a food manufacturer in Tokyo. Even there it was Nakamura who persuaded the company to allow Seko the time off 'to help him become the top runner in the world'.

Nakamura is a millionaire businessman who retired in his early 50s to concentrate on his passion for coaching. He is a former Japanese 1,500 metres record holder himself but was away from the sport for almost 15 years after retiring from the track.

Now he is a track coach at an exclusive private college in Tokyo's Waseda University, paid a nominal 150 dollars annually. The money is irrelevant to him. He spends 15,000 dollars of his own on his runners every year; part on feeding them foods such as steak which are too expensive for them to buy themselves and part on training trips abroad. Seko has spent up to a month in New Zealand in each of the past three years.

He recruited Seko initially when he arrived at Waseda, noting his smooth and relaxed running style. 'If you do what I tell you,' he said, 'you'll become one of the world's greatest marathoners in a few years.'

Since Seko was a high school 800 and 1,500 runner, it was an extraordinary prediction. Seko was also undisciplined and lazy in training and it was liable to remain unfulfilled. When his parents had paid for him to spend six months training with the University of Southern California track team, he had done so little that he returned home 20 pounds heavier!

But Seko became Nakamura's ultimate challenge. Soon he had pushed his training up to 25 miles a day. He insisted that Seko live with him and his wife 'to prepare him mentally'. His hairstyle is straight out of the US Marines, World War II variety. His lifestyle is right out of a monastery. 'The marathon is my only girlfriend,' he says.

Before the 1981 Boston he ran one 80 km training stint (50 miles), running non-stop for six hours. When he broke the world 30 km record a month before that, he sliced more than two minutes off a time which had stood for 11 years. But he also holds the Japanese 10,000 metres record at 27:43.5, a time bettered among the marathon elite only by Alberto Salazar and Craig Virgin. So he is no slouch on the track.

But in Japan it is the marathon which means the most. The marathoner today is the *samurai*, the man who lives and fights with honour. Nakamura has interpreted the *bushido*, the way of the warrior; his *Zensoho* is his way. But others there do the same. The Soh brothers, Shigeru and Takeshi, Seko's closest rivals, also live with their coach in a parental relationship.

The commitment pays. Japan is a relatively weak nation in track and field events but at the marathon it is supreme. Four Japanese ran 1:10:23 or better in the Fukuoka race in 1980, all four ranking in the world's top ten that year. Whether East Germany would have won the Olympic marathon that year but for Japan's boycott will also remain an open question.

Waldemar Cierpinski

The bunch at the front after 15 miles of the 1976 Olympic marathon were a talented crowd. Leading was the defending Olympic champion Frank Shorter. With him were the 1975 Boston winner Bill Rodgers, the 1975 Fukuoka winner Jerome Drayton, the 1972 Olympic silver medallist Karel Lismont and the incredible Lasse

Viren making his debut in a marathon having already won the 5,000 and 10,000 metres in Montreal.

It was the sort of field bookmakers offer odds on and dismiss the rest with a 'bar these five'. There was, however, a sixth; a shortish man in an all-white strip whom nobody knew and few bothered with. Had the other runners had the chance to consult their programmes they would not have worried. He had at best not broken 2:12:20 for the distance.

Shorter admitted he did not like the look of him. 'I felt I had all the guys beat, except one,' he said later. 'I didn't know his name. Or his country. In fact, for a while I thought he was Carlos Lopes of Portugal. But when the strain was showing on the faces of the other guys, he still looked fresh and impassive.'

'I wasn't frightened because I wasn't in trouble myself. There was just the vivid realisation that this unknown runner was so impressive.'

Shorter was surging now to break up the leaders. One by one they dropped back. All except one. At one point Shorter had a 30 metre lead on him and then was reeled back. At 30 km there was a counter surge and Shorter was gone. Within 5km he was 13 seconds back and at 40km 32 seconds adrift.

At the finish the unknown runner in all-white caught a glimpse of a lap marker indicating a lap to go. He ran on, completing another lap and coming over the line finally at the same time as Shorter. They shook hands as they finished.

Shorter was still no wiser of the man's identity. 'I found out he wasn't Lopes when he came alongside me on the track after the race and said: 'Sprechen Sie Deutsch?' I thought, 'That's a funny thing for a guy from Portugal to say.'

His name was Waldemar Cierpinski, and what he did to the great Frank Shorter, a man who had won the Fukuoka race four times, he was to do again to other great runners in Moscow in 1980 when he became only the second man to win the Olympic marathon title for a second time.

Yet after those four years it was as appropriate for his rivals to ask 'who is he?' as it had been for Shorter in Montreal. Cierpinski was as mysterious then in his performances as he had been when he started.

He was born in 1950 in Neugattersleben, had shown athletic promise as a youngster but never realised it in his specialist steeplechase. Turning to 10,000 metres after winning the East German steeplechase title in 1972, he had an average best of 28:40 by 1974 when he tried his first marathon.

He was third in 2:20:29 in appalling weather conditions, and a year later in the same race improved by three minutes although finishing only seventh. Suddenly in 1976 he won the Karl Marx Stadt race and then blazed to victory in the East German trials in 2:12:22. So considerable was his victory that the selectors decided to send him alone to Montreal and he proved them right.

What has never been proved is whether Cierpinski is a great marathon runner or simply an expert at peaking for a single day in each four year period. Is he another Viren or another Abebe Bikila, who know only one motivation: the Olympic crown?

Consider the evidence. Cierpinski won only seven of his 17 marathons between 1974 and 1980, four of those within East Germany, two at Olympics and the other an uncompetitive race in Czechoslovakia. He ran four times in Fukuoka, the most competitive marathon outside the Olympics, and his best place was third in 1976, immediately after his first Olympic win.

In 1978 there, he had finished among the also-rans, in 1979 he had dropped out and in 1980, after winning the Olympics again, was sixth, admittedly in the second best time of his life at 2:10:24.

Consider, too, his other performances between the two Olympics. In 1977 he was only third in the Kosice race in 2:16, and was ranked nowhere that year. In 1978, after serious preparations for the European championships, he finished only fourth and in 1979 he was placed only third on East Germany's own domestic marathon rankings. Indeed in the years between the Olympics he had not risen above 12th on the world rankings and never bettered 2:12.

There were many, of course, who argued that he would never have won a second time had the Japanese and Americans not boycotted the Moscow Games. Significantly when he came up against the Japanese in Fukuoka four months later four of them beat him.

But Cierpinski dismisses these accusations. When presented

Waldemar Cierpinski

with Japanese newspaper headlines that claimed the Fukuoka race was an Olympic decider between Toshihiko Seko and himself, Cierpinski said: 'That's ridiculous. Like Lasse Viren, I train exclusively for the ultimate: the Olympic gold medal. Other races are merely steps along the way in my preparation.'

That was how it had happened. After his mediocre year in 1979, he had resumed in 1980 with victory in the East German trials in his second fastest time, and then in a world class field, even without the Americans and Japanese — 13 of the world's fastest 20 of that year were in it.

He ran it just as he had in 1976 with his willingness to allow others to set the pace for 25 kilometres. At one stage he was 49 seconds behind the Mexican Rudolfo Gomez's suicidal pace. But by 35 km he was only three seconds behind Gomez. 'I felt that I began to feel a little bit sure of victory at that point,' he said.

It was not easy. He admitted that the last two kilometres were 'painful', and although he sprinted the last lap of the stadium — his final 200 metres in only 33.4 seconds — he beat the Dutchman Gerard Nijboer by only 17 seconds. It did not fully answer the question about the intervening years but at least it proved that when it came to the ultimate test, he was the champion.

John Graham

The first London marathon established a mountain of marathoners in Britain but the man who should be at its peak is doubled up at the metaphorical roadside. John Graham, as one writer put it, is 'just a stitch away from stardom'.

Stitch afflicts all and nobody runs through it. Suffer it in a marathon and only the easing of your pace will tame the breathtaking pain in your side. Some suffer it because they eat too soon before a run. Some suffer when they drink before a race, others when they do not. There are those who suffer inexplicably. John Graham is one of them.

By the simple measurement of the clock John Graham is the best of the young generation of British marathoners. Only Ian Thompson, back in his glorious year of 1974, has ever run faster among the British and only six men in the world have surpassed his time of 2:09:28. By the yardstick of consistency, Graham is nowhere. Too often after his name, where the placing should be, are the salutary letters 'dnf'.

He has run nine marathons and failed to finish four. One of those, the AAA championship at Rugby in 1981, was a deliberate failure. He had been forced to appear and pulled out after 20 miles when he had completed his usual 20 mile Sunday training run. Two weeks later he ran the fastest race of his life in Rotterdam.

In another, his first, he was beaten by a bout of malaria but the other two were down to stitch, one in New Zealand and the other in the European Cup in Agen. In two others in which he has completed the course, stitch has hampered him. In New York in 1981, when he was struck by it, he slumped from the halfway lead to 44th. In Rotterdam it cost him the world record.

He felt it first there after 30km. He was 14 seconds inside Derek Clayton's schedule, and storming it. Suddenly the pain came. His stride shortened. In the next 5km his pace was 38 seconds slower, the next 5km a minute slower. He rallied to run the last 2,195 metres in 6:18, a blistering pace to finish, but the record was gone.

He has consulted specialists, considered operations and still not discovered what is at the root of it. The most likely cause, he believes, is an injury suffered when playing football in his native Motherwell. 'I went up to head a ball and twisted,' he recalls. 'Perhaps I did something to my diaphragm.'

If Graham could cure it he could be the best there has ever been. He knew that when he finished the Rotterdam race. Stitch and a sea breeze notwithstanding he had missed the world record by little more than two seconds a mile.

Graham, like the Olympic champion Waldemar Cierpinski, is a converted steeplechaser. Unlike the East German, he had no record at 10,000 metres to indicate he could take the giant step up to the marathon.

His best 10km — and almost his only 10km — was run when he was 17 at 30:00. Although he was in the national steeplechase squad in 1979, he never bettered 8:39, and he has never run a sub-four minute mile. But he was good over the country and when he won the Birchfield 10, organised by his own club in 47:49, it was obvious where fate was leading him. All he needed was a qualifying time for the marathon.

That came in spectacular fashion in the North Staffs 20 miles. Conditions were fearful, driving rain and sleet with the roads awash. Yet Graham beat class marathon runners such as Trevor Wright and Andy Holden in 1:39:14, under five minute miling, and he did it having lost 100 yards going back to retrieve his hat!

He failed to finish his first marathon, the 1980 AAA, because of the after effects of the malaria he had first contracted at the Commonwealth Games in 1978. His second he won in Spain — becoming Spanish champion — and in the third in Eugene he ran out of steam after setting a 4:40 pace too soon and finishing only eighth. In his fourth he was third in New York, holding the leaders for the first 20 miles.

Clearly there is considerably more to come. The marathon itself is nothing more than the distance Graham's whole running life has been leading him towards since he was 15. He ran for 2¾ hours at that age, and at 16 was training 70 miles a week. 'When I was 13 some of the lads in my Boys' Brigade threatened to bang my head unless I lapped them!'

He moved south to Birmingham with his wife Alyson after the 1979 track season, and since he has never managed to combine work and running, she supports him totally from her wages as a catering manageress. With the day to himself he has time for three training sessions, and has pushed his weekly mileage to an average of 130 with a peak of nearer 150. 'Running is full-time, even overtime,' he says. And for him work begins each day as early as 7.30 with his first run. 'My running is my job.'

Unfortunately he is labouring under a handicap. Stitch does not only affect his racing but his training. It can occur at any time. In Agen he had only been running for four miles when it struck him. In training it can come on within minutes of starting.

'When I did that soccer injury,' he says in his thick Scottish accent, 'it was just a torn muscle in my side. I didn't do anything about it and it healed naturally. Or so I thought. Something has got to be wrong though. I've tried everything to cure it. I never need to drink during a race, so after Agen I ran a 30km in Stockholm and took drinks for the first time. That was fine, and I won. But in New York, it happened all over again.'

'I am not frightened of anybody in the marathon. I could not really get out of running Agen for Britain in September but it came in the middle of everything and left me only six weeks to prepare for New York. If I could prepare correctly, in my own way and without this stitch, I could do something special. When you know that, dropping out isn't much fun.'

John Graham

Joyce Smith

Joyce Smith

Like British Rail schedules, Joyce Smith never runs to time. She may have become one of the five fastest women marathoners in history but she has only ever run to win. Aiming for times makes her nervous.

'We've learned from experience that when we talk in terms of times for a race, she suffers a great stress problem,' says Bryan Smith, her coach and husband. 'She just doesn't like to think of what is possible.'

Pre-race talk in the Smith household in Watford, north of London, revolves around tactics and opposition only. Who to beat and how to beat them precludes any mention of the time necessary. Yet Mrs Joyce Smith, mother of two, has nevertheless set the fastest time for a veteran woman and an over-40.

'It just so happens that the races she has gone into hoping to win have had people who have pushed her,' says Bryan. 'I'm not saying we don't know what may be possible, only that it doesn't play a part in our race plans or at least the discussions about them.'

Joyce is the most remarkable of the first generation of marathoners. Not only was she 41 years of age when she ran her first marathon but she went on to win six of her first eight and set British records in five of them, finally breaking through the 2:30 barrier in the 1981 London race, only the third woman ever to do so.

It was not so much a second wind for her athletic's career as a third life. After more than 20 years of trying, starting with long jumping at school and ranging across the sprints, 800, 1,500 and 3,000 metres, she had finally found the right event and carved out a fourth decade as an international runner.

In the 1950s she had won the English national cross-country championship and represented England in the international championship. In 1960 she had represented Britain at 800 metres and, after a 12 year gap, had come back to run for her country again at 1,500 metres, twice breaking the British record and captaining the women's track team at the 1972 Olympics. Two years later, close to her 37th birthday, she had won a bronze medal at 3,000 metres in the European championships.

In those days women were simply not allowed to race as far as even 10 miles in Britain, and she was in her 40th year before she was to run a British best for a woman of 56:27. 'You have to have the basic speed to run fast marathons, and it's all in the progression,' says Bryan. 'You won't run fast marathons without running fast 10s, and you won't run fast 10s before you can run fast 5000s. I would say if a woman cannot break 60 minutes for 10 miles she might as well forget about attempting a fast marathon.'

Joyce's first marathon came about because of an injury which put an end to her international track career and prematurely ended her 1978 season. It was a stress fracture, and she was out of running for nearly three months. When she began training again Bryan prescribed plenty of mileage.

For the first part of the winter she averaged 36 miles each week but after finishing 15th in the national cross-country championship, the new target became her first marathon: the Sandbach Avon in June, 1979.

Her mileage built up until she was averaging 61¼ miles weekly with a high week of 92 miles. She won the marathon in a new British record of 2:41:37. Fourteen weeks later she improved that by five minutes in the Avon International in West Germany. Eight weeks later she won again in Tokyo.

She was disqualified in the Orange Bowl in Miami in January 1980 after collapsing with heat exhaustion (the temperature was in the high 70s and humidity around 93%) and receiving assistance over the finishing line. But in the 1980 Sandbach race she was pushed by Swiss girl Vreni Forster to another British record of 2:33:32.

Illness and injury hampered her preparations for the 1980 Avon International race through London and she was happy to finish seventh, but in the 15 weeks before the 1980 Tokyo race she was able to average 71 miles a week. This time she knocked three minutes off her British record and in the first London the following March, she cracked that 2:30 barrier.

Joyce calculates training monthly. She runs three weeks hard, and one week with the throttle eased back. So in the hard weeks she will average 85 miles and in the fourth week around 75, and each marathon build-up takes 12 weeks. For just two of those weeks her mileage might peak around 100.

The typical week is – Monday: morning 8 miles. Tuesday: morning 6 miles, evening 3 × 1 mile with 400 metres jog between or 4 × 800 metres with the same interval. Wednesday: 15 miles (rising to 20 three weeks before race). Thursday: morning 8 miles, evening 9 miles. Friday: 6 or 9 depending whether racing next day. Saturday: Run morning if racing afternoon but nothing if travelling for race; 18 miles if no race. Sunday: 10 miles. Saturday's run will be 25 miles for last three weeks. She is on her own for all those runs except for the speed session on Tuesday when she pairs off with another of Bryan's group, Sharon Harvey, a 1,500 and 3,000 metres specialist. 'Joyce carries a watch with her on all her runs and tries to keep it around six minute mile pace,' says Bryan. 'But we've never measured the distances, so they could be slightly more or less than we think.'

Bryan never allows her to run beyond the marathon distance, and there is a firm conviction that speed work is important. After a marathon, Joyce will do much more speed training until the next 12 week build-up begins.

'Now the marathon is in the Olympics, there will be many 3,000 metres runners thinking of trying it, and I think that will keep the women's event progressing. Overall, women are at their limit at about 90 per cent of men's times. In the marathon they're a little short still of 85 per cent. So there's room for improvement but I'd guess that while the men's record is around 2:8 the women's won't get better than 2:20. It's going to start coming down in 10-20-30 second bursts, not as Greta Waitz did.'

What are Joyce's prospects as she enters her 45th year? 'She missed most of 1981 because of injury, and she didn't want to end on a blank year,' says Bryan. 'So we've planned a build-up towards the first European marathon championship, and after that we'll have to wait and see.'

Bill Rodgers

Bill Rodgers remembers the time he was not the world's best marathon runner. He was rooming with Amby Burfoot, who was to win the Boston in 1968. Rodgers was a sophomore, Burfoot a senior. Burfoot dragged him to races.

'I remember this 13 miler Amby got me to run once in February. It was snowing and very cold. A very strategic part of my anatomy just about froze. It was agonising and I kept thinking, "This is insane".'

The same insanity has since made Bill Rodgers a very rich man. In the years since Burfoot had to drag him protesting to any start line, he has won the Boston four times, the New York four times and has set an American record. He has become the owner of three shops bearing his name, a line of running clothes and writes a column in a running magazine. He gives clinics, after-dinner speeches and dines with the President.

Rodgers today is not so much a runner as an industry, and in 1980 it earned him around 250,000 dollars before tax. Incredibly it has not changed his thinking. 'Racing isn't fun. Well, it's half fun and half hellish. It is an intense challenge physically and psychologically. If you want to test your limits, it's great for that. It's such a grind, training and running year in and year out. It's a hard lifestyle.'

It was not a lifestyle he chose consciously. As a child in Connecticut, he ran chasing butterflies. He ran round blocks, through parks, anywhere. Nobody took it seriously. His mother recalls their high school coach, when asked how Bill was progressing with his running, saying, 'I wouldn't get too excited about his prospects'.

Nobody did. He was a classic drifter; smoking, leaving college to take a job delivering mail and then seeking conscientious objector status when the Vietnam draft threatened, He also stopped running. When his CO status came through and he was forced to take a special job, he worked at Peter Bent Brigham Hospital in Boston and spent his evenings in bars.

He started running again after he met his future wife Ellen. She encouraged him to run in the 1973 Boston marathon. Every runner did in Boston. The marathon is Boston as much as the Tea Party and the Red Sox. He did not finish. For the next year he trained harder, and finished 14th; the last but one in the race to beat 2:20. He was 26 seconds inside it. A year later he won the marathon in a record time. The era of Rodgers had begun.

In his home city he became Boston Billy, the greatest thing that had ever run on two legs. To the finish announcer at Boston in 1979 when he won the race a third time he was 'the greatest distance runner in the history of the world'. To Frank Shorter, the man he succeeded as the best American runner, he is 'the best guy in the world, maybe the best ever'.

His record supports these claims. He had run 31 marathons when he won in Stockholm in the summer of 1981, and won 19 of them, 21 in a time faster than 2:20; more than any other American had run. He had run the Boston for three consecutive years and New York for four years; and over the winter of 1977-78 he became the only man to win New York, Fukuoka and Boston in succession.

So he was all of the things they say he was but is he now? Alberto Salazar prompted the question in New York in October,

Bill Rodgers

1980 but Rodgers fell and was brave to come back to fifth place.

Toshihiko Seko posed the same question the following spring on Rodgers' own roads in Boston. Rodgers finished second to him but then again the American had suffered flu a month before the race and had to cut his training by half for a fortnight.

Finally though in New York in 1981 the question could not be asked because at the eleventh hour he pulled out of the race when the sponsors would not agree his terms. He had won Boston and Toronto in 1980 but for the first time since 1974 had not been ranked number one in his own country. In 1981 he has only won Stockholm and would be lucky to be ranked in the first five in America.

Rodgers had seen the challenge coming as far back as 1979 when he was winning the third Boston. 'I've had a streak, and I'm into my prime years but it ain't gonna last for ever', he said at the time.

Rodgers ran too often to last forever. He was regularly lining up for 30 races each year; anything from 10,000 metres to a marathon. On top of that his fame as a runner increased the demands on him as a businessman. In little more than a year he was earning 10 times his 1977 salary as a teacher, and that required considerably harder work.

He had also always had a weak achilles heel and was vulnerable to the heat. With his fair hair and fair skin, he really suffered. Three times in his career he has failed to finish a marathon, and apart from the first at Boston when he was not ready, the others at Enschede and Boston in 1977 were in temperatures exceeding 25C. 'I lose my desire to run in the heat', he once said.

Fortunately he has not yet lost his desire to run on other days. The rise of Rodgers paralleled the rise of running. Someday road runners will happily take prize money, but even with excessive expenses, appearance money and cash prizes still ruled out for amateurs, Rodgers had profited very well.

But how much longer can he continue the grind of training and running year in and year out? One week in 1979 when he was still on that streak he ran 170 miles. Often he was pushing 145, not far short of a daily marathon. He recognises the inevitable: 'I'm not going to do 120 miles a week all my life. I will retire some day. Being the best 41 year old in the world won't motivate me sufficiently'.

His old rival Frank Shorter reckons both he and Rodgers will be around in 1984 to challenge for Olympic places but there are now many more runners coming through to challenge them both. Nobody passed Boston Billy for a long long while but Time now has him beat on the inside track.

Bill Bull

The white van, the rack on its roof a reminder of another sport at another time, is plastered now with slogans of a new love. 'I've run a marathon', boasts one. 'I love NY', admits another.

The two are complimentary, and Bill Bull, self-employed carpenter, is happy that friends, neighbours and potential customers in the suburban haven of Sutton, south of London, know it. Today's marathoners are long since out of the closet.

Bill Bull spent half his life trying to get into Britain's Olympic teams. In 1960 he came so close that he was a reserve for the British eight which rowed in Rome. Twice more, in the Seventies, he was in the canoe team's training squad before the games.

Now he is a marathoner, and the determination is evident again. A four hour marathon may not seem so high a mountain as Olympus but it is driving him as hard. 'When I packed in canoeing, I promised my wife Jean that that was it. I was finished with sport', he says. At 46 he was hardly in the first flush of youth.

'She was delighted. You can imagine . . . all those evenings on her own, those things she had to do for the kids because I wasn't there, all the frustrations when I didn't make it. And it was over. She's put up with a lot for 20 odd years, and now no more.'

That decision was reversed after an evening out running with a journalist friend, David Emery. Bill still had hopes then of making the canoe team for Moscow but they were slim. 'If you don't make the team, how about the two of us running the New York marathon', Emery had suggested.

'It was about five months away then, and seemed a good idea at the time. I was pretty fit anyway, and five months, I thought, should be enough. I can remember Jean saying "Oh, no, not again'' but I assured her it was only a temporary thing, that after New York I'd pack it in again.'

The two of them averaged 20 miles a week at first, and then stepped it up to 30. All was going well seven weeks before the race when Bill had to have a minor operation on his feet. It was nothing to do with his running and was not too serious but it left his training diary empty for 10 days.

'It all became a mad rush after that. On the Sunday before the race, we did a 10 mile, then a 15 on the Tuesday and a 12 on the Wednesday and then flew to New York on Thursday. I thought I was pretty fit anyway, so I'd get through. I never imagined that it would be so hard.

'It was good fun at first. You were carried along by the general euphoria. I can remember the cry going up that Rodgers had fallen, and Dave asking: ''How's the horse?'' It was all a bit of a lark. Then we heard that Salazar had finished and Dave said ''Christ, do you realise we've still two hours to go'' and then it started to sink in what was ahead. The last six miles was like starting all over again. One of my friends had warned me that 20 miles is only half way and I'd dismissed it. But he was right. My knees! I can't tell you the pain. I dragged myself into the finish. Only sheer determination to get there forced me to finish. I felt I couldn't go all that way and fail. David finished in 4:25 and I did 4:28. At the finish we swore we'd never do anything so stupid again.

'Strange how quickly the mood changed. The same evening we were in Charley O's bar celebrating our great triumph and discussing where we'd run next, Paris, Stockholm, London . . . There and then we formed the 26:2 Road Runners Club made up of five members. Suddenly it all seemed very serious. I couldn't stop. It was in the blood.'

Bill Bull, 46 when he ran his first marathon and hanging a muscular 175 lb frame in his 5 ft 10 inches, had never been a runner. A run in his long sporting experience was the three miles or so you did to warm up before getting in the boat. What minute mile pace you did was as immaterial to a Thames boatman as the tide fall on the Pontiac.

But on November 17, 1981, three weeks after his first marathon, he wrote the first entry in a runner's diary: 'Five miles, ran with Mike Morgan, 45 minutes'. The target now was London, March 29 of the following year and that four hour barrier.

Twenty weeks and 600 miles later he was better prepared than he had been for New York but the average was not high enough to be confident. He had gone beyond 60 in a week on occasions but had missed more than a week with flu and another with achilles tendon pain, and the achilles was not wholly cured. 'I was running well for 10 miles and then the achilles went. I hobbled the rest. I was well sick', he recalls.

But he had improved to 4:16:55, 11 minutes up on New York, and the 26.2 Club had grown to 17 members by London all of whom had finished. Next came the Horsham 10 in 74 minutes and then the Dartford Half-Marathon in 1 hour 43 minutes but all were leading back to the start again across the Verrazano-Narrows Bridge on October 25.

The Pony Greater Manchester marathon was used only as a training run but he pushed his best to 4:15:18. 'The last six were bloody slow, around 12 minute miles, all up hill. I hope NY is better', he wrote in his diary. He was now averaging more than 50 miles each week, and three weeks before New York pushed it beyond 70 for the first time. With two weeks to go he clocked up his 978th mile since London. He was hoping, he wrote in the diary, for 3:40.

At the start, he reckoned, he lost 2½ minutes and another three over the first three miles weaving through runners who had been over-optimistic about their pace.

'What you notice in New York is the state of the roads, all broken up and rough. One lad from the club, Keith Shaw, went down one pothole and broke his arm. He had it strapped there and then and carried on to run 4:20. But the roads do slow you up.'

At 10 miles he was on schedule in 80 minutes, and by the Queensboro Bridge at 15 miles he was five minutes ahead. 'The crowd that greets you coming under the bridge into First Avenue is like running out at Wembley Stadium. Unbelievable. You float down that street.'

At 20 miles he was 10 minutes up on his target. 'I was feeling good for a 3:30 finish but just 300 yards later going over Willis Avenue Bridge, my ankle went. I was slowed to a shuffle. It was sickening, not just the pain of it but the thought that I'd done 2,000 miles since last time here, all the work the other lads had done to get me faster, the 6am runs, the wind, the rain and snow. In the end I had to run the last mile in under 10 minutes to break four hours and could only manage 11 minutes 28 seconds.'

He cannot quit now. 'Running's such a personal thing. Nobody knew or cared how I felt to be just 1 minute 28 seconds outside four hours. It didn't matter that we'd wasted 2½ minutes getting started. When the results were published next day there it was – 9288th in 4:01:28. You can't argue with the official results.'

Now it is London again, and marathon number five and perhaps this time he will make it. The 'temporary thing' has now become a lifestyle, and Jean, recognising the inevitable, has taken up running too.

CHAPTER 9

Running Directory

RUNNING BODIES (and clubs)

Amateur Athletic Association

Francis House, Francis Street, London SW1P 1DL (01-828 9326). Governing body of the sport in England and Wales. Men's races should be run under their rules and with their sanction. Guardians of the amateur rules. No English club runner may race abroad without their written permission, and race organisers abroad may ask to see that permission. Promote annual championship for marathon. Women's AAA, at same address (01-828 4731). Has the same responsibilities for women in England only. Welsh Women's AAA, 19 Coed Bach, Highlight Estate, Barry. Responsibility within that country.

Scottish Amateur Athletic Association

16 Royal Crescent, Glasgow G3 7SL (041-332 5144).
Serves the same function north of the border as its English counterpart. The Scottish Women's AAA is at the same address (041-332 9304).

The Athletic Congress of the USA

PO Box 120, 155 Washington Street, Indianapolis, Indiana 46206 (317-638 9155).
Serves the same function as its English counterpart but is affiliated directly to the International Amateur Athletic Federation (domestic organisations in Britain afiliate through the British Amateur Athletic Board).

British Area Associations

Southern Counties AAA, Francis House, Francis Street, London SW1P 1DL (01-828 8640).

Midland Counties AAA, Devonshire House, High Street, Deritend, Birmingham B12 0LP (021-773 1631).

Northern Counties AAA, Studio 44, Bluecoat Chambers, School Lane, Liverpool L1 3BX (051-708 9363).

Northern Ireland AAA, men: 20 Kernan Park, Portadown, Co. Armagh; women: 8 Broadway Avenue, Ballymena.

Road Runners Club of America
c/o Jeff Darman, 2737 Devonshire Place, NW Washington DC 20008 or Stuart J. Brahs, 803 Brice Road, Rockville, MD 20852. Serves the interest of the long distance runner. Transplanted from its British original in 1958. Originally under the presidency of ultra-marathon star Ted Corbitt. Produces quarterly newsletter, and oversees hundreds of marathons, all certified to the right measurement by its Standards Committee.

Road Runners Club
10 Honeywood Road, Colchester, Essex (0206 74637).
Aims to bring together all those interested in long distance running. Organises members' marathon championship annually and other road races. Members receive comprehensive list of all road races over 10 miles, and full accident insurance while training or racing. Responsible for compilation of all world records over 30 kilometres. Membership (cost £1 per year) open only to those already members of clubs affiliated to the AAA/WAAA. Publishes it own newsletter three times yearly.

The British Marathon Runners Club
13 Albany Road, Old Windsor, Berkshire (Windsor 62527).
Objectives are to raise the standard of marathon running in Britain, to improve the knowledge of runners and coaches and to ensure that full advantage is taken of international competitions. Originally had severely restricted membership limited to elite but it is now open to men who have bettered three hours and women who have bettered 3:30. Lesser qualifications for veterans. Certain coaches and invited experts are also members. An organisation which has opened its doors wider in recent days, and welcomes non-members to occasional one-day training coaching sessions.

Scottish Marathon Club
8 Craig Road, Glasgow G44 3DR (041-633 2236).
Aims to foster and promote long distance running and races. Membership is open to any amateur runner. Promotes club

championship races, including marathon, and a standards scheme.

Stone Master Marathoners

The Radfords, Stone, Staffordshire (0785 814120).

Claims to be the only veterans' marathon club in the world. Has a national membership exclusively among those men over 35 and women over 30, open to novices and elite, in Britain or abroad. Organises its own Flying Fox marathon for veterans and takes groups to many leading foreign races.

Spiridon Club of Great Britain

10 Maple Rise, Marlow, Buckinghamshire (06284 74767).

Part of the European Spiridon movement (derives its name from that of the first Olympic marathon champion) which seeks to promote all forms of running from 800 meters up. Has 300 members and would welcome more veterans, more women and more fun runners. Excellent source of information on courses abroad, travel arrangements and its members are often invited abroad. Membership open to all but members must be attached to another club to race as Spiridon is not affiliated to the AAA.

London Road Runners Club

6 Upper Montague Street, London W1.

Membership open to all those interested in road running in the capital. Affiliated to AAA and WAAA but seeks to complement existing athletic clubs, promoting road races only and offering comprehensive information services on UK road running scene. Strong on social side and reckons three-quarters of its present membership has never been involved in athletic's club system.

New York Road Runners Club

PO Box 881, FDR Station, New York 10150.

Has its own headquarters on East 89th Street and is probably the world's largest athletics club with more than 20,000 members. Membership open to all, whatever their nationality and fees are according to home residence. Publishes a regular magazine and comprehensive road running fixture lists, and is active in the organisation of training nights and more than 200 competitions including, of course, the famous New York City marathon each October. Membership does not guarantee you entry into that race.

Dolphin South End Runners
c/o Dolphin Club, Fisherman's Wharf, San Francisco, 94127.
San Francisco's oldest and largest running club. Founded in 1966, and non-competitive in philosophy. Offshoot in 1966 of century-old Dolphin Swimming and Boating club in Fisherman's Wharf overlooking Bay. Welcomes out-of-towners. Publishes newsletter.

The Boston Athletic Association
John Cedarholm, 180 Beacon Street, Boston, Mass 01867.
Oldest club in the United States and largely responsible for US success in first modern Olympics. Organises the annual Boston marathon. Club membership open to men and women.

RUNNING GEAR

These shops specialise in running equipment, and are able to offer specialist advice as well as a mail order service.

Britain

Bourne Sports, Church Street, Stoke-on-Trent, ST4 1DJ (0782 410411).
Bernie Plain Sports, 6 Four Elms Road, Roath, Cardiff (0222 492520).
The Sweat Shop, The Causeway, Teddington, Middlesex TW11 0HF (01-943 0239).
Running Wild, 2 Tower Street, Hyde, Cheshire (061-368 8008).
Warstock Sports & Leisure, 251 Highters Heath Lane, Birmingham B14 4NX (021-430 8445).

United States

Bill Rodgers Running Centre, 372A Chestnut Hill, Boston 02146.
Athletic Attic, 1170 Third, New York 10021.
Inside Track, 1410 East Main, Ventura, CA 93001.
Philippides of Oregon, 445 High Street, SE, Salem 97301.
Garry Bjorklund Sports, 831 Marquette, Minneapolis 55402.

RUNNING BOOKS

There are scores on the market which mention the marathon in one way or another but this selection is recommended.

Aerobics, Dr Kenneth Cooper (Bantam)

Boston, America's Oldest Marathon, ed. Ray Hosler (Anderson World, 1400 Stierlin Road, Mountain View, CA 94043)

The Challenge Of The Marathon, Cliff Temple (Stanley Paul, London)

The Complete Jogger, Bruce Tulloh (Pan, London)

The Complete Marathoner, ed. Joe Henderson (Anderson World)

The Complete Book Of Running, James Fixx (Random House)

Jim Fixx's Second Book Of Running (Random House)

The Marathon Footrace, David Martin & Roger Gynn (Charles C. Thomas, Springfield, Illinois)

Runner's Handbook, Bob Glover & Jack Shepherd (Penguin)

The Runner's Log (Runner's Log, 10-50, Jackson Ave, Long Island City, NY 11101)

The Runners' Repair Manual, Dr Murray Weisenfeld & Barabara Burr (W.H. Allen, London)

A Scientific Approach To Distance Running, Dr David Costill (Tafnews Press, Box 296, Los Altos, CA 94022)

Target 26, Skip Brown & John Graham (Collier Books)

Running To The Top, Derek Clayton (Anderson World)

Marathoning, Manfred Steffney (Anderson World)

RUNNING MAGAZINES

Britain

Athletics Weekly, 344 High Street, Rochester, Kent ME1 1DT (Weekly)

Running, 5-8 Lower John Street, London W1 (Monthly)

America

The Runner, PO Box 2730, Boulder, Colorado 80322 (Monthly)

Runner's World, 1400 Stierlin Road, Mountain View, CA 94043 (Monthly)

Running, PO Box 10990, 1508 Oak Street, Eugene, Oregon 97440 (Monthly)

Track And Field News, Box 296, Los Altos, CA 94022. (Monthly)

New Zealand

New Zealand Runner, 72 Grafton Road, Auckland I, New Zealand (Bi-monthly).

RUNNING REPAIRS

This is the latest list of sports injury clinics, operating within the British National Health Service, as supplied by the Sports Council. Please note that you should be referred to a clinic by your GP, rather than approaching the hospital direct.

Aldershot: Cambridge Military Hospital (0252 22521 Ext 208) Lt. B.L. Wilcox.

Bedford: Bedford Hospital (0234 55122) Dr Hawkes.

Birmingham: Accident Hospital and Rehabilitation Centre (021-643 7041) Mr Nigel Tubbs.
General Hospital, Steelhouse Lane (021-236 8611) Mr J.R. Pearson.

Bristol: Royal Infirmary (0272 22041) Mr P.G. Stableforth.

Cambridge: Addenbrookes Hospital (0223 45151 Ext 254) Dr Sylvia Lachmann.

Colchester: Severalls Hospital (soft tissue only) (0206 77271) Dr Gilbert.

Derby: Derbyshire Royal Infirmary (0332 47141 Ext 556) Dr George M. Cochrane.

Glasgow: Victoria Infirmary (041-649 4545) Mr A. McDougall.

Guildford: St Luke's Hospital (0483 71122) Dr Malcolm Read.

Kettering: District General Hospital (soft tissue only) (0536 81141) Dr I.M. Morris and Dr P.C. Matingley.

Leeds: St James Hospital (0532 33144) Dr Ian Adams.

London: Guy's Hospital (01-407 7600 Ext 2424) Dr Terence Gibson and Dr John E. Davies.
Hackney Hospital (01-985 5555) Dr R. Neil Baxter.

King's College Hospital, Denmark Hill (01-274 6222 Ext 2434) Rheumatology and Rehabilitation: Mr J.G. Jones.
The Middlesex Hospital, Mortimore Street (01-636 8333) Mr Alan F. Bedford.
Royal Northern Hospital, Mortimore Street (01-272 7777) Mr Martin Lowy.
St Charles Hospital, Exmoor Street (01-969 2488) Dr Leonard Sash.
Westminster Hospital (01-828 9811) Dr Ian Curwen.

Northampton: Northampton General Hospital (0604 34700) Dr T.C. Beer and Dr F.A. Newton.

Slough: Farnham Park Rehabilitation Centre (369-2271)
Dr John Williams.

Southampton: General Hospital (0703 777222).

Uxbridge: Hillingdon Hospital (0895 38282) Dr Peter Sperryn.

Weymouth: District Hospital (03057 72211)

In Oswestry the Institute of Orthopaedics (0691 5311) and in Oxford the Nuffield Orthopaedic Centre (0865 64811) will also treat sports injuries.

RUNNING THROUGH THE YEARS

CHRONOLOGICAL HISTORY OF THE MARATHON

April 10 1896 First Olympic marathon, Marathon to Athens, 40km, is won by Spiridon Louis (Greece) at 7 min 11.8 seconds per mile pace. Nine runners started.

September 9 1896 First New York marathon, Stamford, Conn. to Columbia Oval, 25 miles, is won by New Yorker John McDermott.

October 4 1896 First Norwegian marathon, 40.2 km, won by Hallstein Bjerke, 28 runners; first Hungarian marathon won by Bela Janko, 40km.

April 19 1897 First Boston marathon, Metcalfe's Mill, Ashland, to Irvington Oval, 24.7 miles, is won by John McDermott at 7:05.5 per mile pace.

1897 World's first national marathon championship run in Norway, 40.2 km, won by Hallstein Bjerke.

1898 First marathon in Germany, 40 km, won by Arthur Techtow.

1904 Third Olympic marathon in St Louis. USA take all three medals (only time in Olympic history). Winner is Thomas Hicks, only English-born runner ever to win Olympic marathon.

1905 Fred Lorz, banned by AAU 'for life' for taking a ride during 1904 Olympics, is reinstated and wins the Boston marathon.

1906 An 18-year-old, Timothy Ford, wins the Boston.

1907 Thomas Longboat (Canada) runs first sub-6 min mile pace at Boston (5:50.8).

1908 First South African national championships, Cape Town, is won by Kenneth McArthur.

July 24 1908 First marathon over now-standard distance of 26 miles 385 yards at London Olympics, from Windsor Castle to White City. American John Hayes awarded gold medal after Italian Dorando Pietri is disqualified for receiving assistance.

October 1908 First professional marathon in US.

April 1909 Boston: 91 of the 164 starters fail to finish.

May 8 1909 First Polytechnic Harriers marathon, 26 miles, 385 yards, Windsor Park to Stamford Bridge, won by club member Harry Barrett.

August 1909 First Australian championship, Brisbane.

November 1909	AAU of America ban children under 16 from running races over five miles and demand medical examination of all contestants.
December 1909	Illinois Athletic Club cancel annual marathon because of 'health risk'.
July 14 1912	Fifth Olympic marathon in Stockholm is first to have regular watering points but Portugal's Francisco Lazaro becomes first fatality.
May 12 1913	Harry Green (Britain) runs first sub-2 hour 40 minute time (2:38:16.2) for full distance, in London.
1920	Antwerp Olympics. Longest ever marathon at the Games of 42.75 km. Won by Finn Johannes Kolehmainen in first Olympic time to better six minute miling pace.
1924	International Olympic Committee direct that all Olympic marathons will be 26 miles 385 yards (42.195 km).
1925	Boston nominated as official US national championships; Poly named as official British championships. First German marathon championship in Leipzig.
1925	First sub 2 hour 30 min marathon (2:29:11.8) in Port Chester by American Al 'Whitey' Michelsen.
October 3 1926	First known marathon by a woman, Violet Piercy, Chiswick, London, in 3:40:22.0. Not part of race.
1928	Sam Ferris (Britain) wins Poly for fourth consecutive year. First African, Boughera El Ouafi, (born Ould-Djleb, Algeria, but running for France) wins Olympic marathon in Amsterdam.
1933	Sam Ferris retires after winning eighth Poly race (and 12 of his 19 marathons).
1936	Berlin Olympic marathon was won by Kitei Son (Japan), a native of Korea, in first Olympic sub-2½hour time.

1947 First Asahi marathon at Kumamoto, Japan. The race moved to present course at Fukuoka first in 1957 and premanently in 1964.

1948 Delfo Cabrera (Argentina) wins Olympics in London in marathon debut.

1950 Jack Holden (Britain) wins AAA, Commonwealth and European titles in same year.

1950 Koreans take all three medal places at Boston.

1952 Emil Zatopek (Czechoslovakia) wins Olympic marathon in debut.

1953 Jim Peters (Britain) records first sub-2 hour 20 min time on Windsor-Chiswick course, measured at 156 yards too long. In next two years he ran first four sub-2 hour 20 min times.

1955 First International Classical marathon, Marathon to Athens.

1960 Abebe Bikila (Ethiopia) sets world best time 2:15:16.2 in winning Rome Olympics.

December 1962 Leonard 'Buddy' Edelen becomes first American to run sub-2 hour 20 min at Fukuoka (2:18:56.8).

June 1963 Edelen sets world best (2:14:28) in 50th Windsor-Chiswick Poly marathon.

1963 A woman, Merry Lepper, runs 3:37:03 in Culver City race.

1964 A woman, Dale Greig, runs 3:27:45, at Ryde, Isle of Wight, setting off four minutes before men's race.

1966 First woman, Roberta Gibb Bingay, contests Boston unofficially, 3:21:40.

1967 First woman, Katherine Switzer, runs Boston with official number (261).

1967 First Karl Marz Stadt marathon in East Germany, on enclosed parkland.

December 1967 Derek Clayton (Australia) becomes first sub-2 hour 10 min runner (2:09:36.4) in Fukuoka. First sub-five minute mile marathon.

1969	First field of 1,000 plus at Boston (largest in world).
May 30 1969	Clayton runs world best of 2:08:33.6 at Antwerp.
1970	First New York marathon.
1971	Woman breaks three hour barrier (2:46.30) Adrienne Beames (Australia) at Victoria, Australia.
October 21 1979	Greta Waitz (Norway) becomes the first sub-2½ hour woman (2:27:32.6) when winning the New York race (women) for second consecutive year.
February 21 1981	International Olympic Committee Executive Board vote to include a women's marathon for first time in 1984 Olympics in Los Angeles.
March 29 1981	First London marathon results in a dead-heat for first place. 6,700 starters.
September 1982	First women's marathon in European championships, Athens.

RUNNING'S ROLL OF HONOUR (marathon)

Olympic Champions

Date	Runner	Nation	Time
1896	Spiridon Louis	Greece	**2:58:50**
1900	Michel Theato	France	**2:59:45**
1904	Thomas Hicks	USA	**2:28:53**
1908	John Hayes	USA	**2:55:18.4**
1912	Kenneth McArthur	S. Africa	**2:36:54.8**
1920	Johannes Kolehmainen	Finland	**2:32:35.8**
1924	Albin Stenroos	Finland	**2:41:21.6**
1928	Boughera El Ouafi	France	**2:32:57**

1932	Juan Carlos Zabala	Argentina	**2:31:36**
1936	Kitei Son	Japan	**2:29:19.2**
1948	Delfo Cabrera	Argentina	**2:34:51.6**
1952	Emil Zatopek	Czechoslovakia	**2:23:03.2**
1956	Alain Mimoun	France	**2:25:00**
1960	Abebe Bikila	Ethiopia	**2:15:16.2**
1964	Abebe Bikila	Ethiopia	**2:12:11.2**
1968	Mamo Wolde	Ethiopia	**2:20:26.4**
1972	Frank Shorter	USA	**2:12:19.8**
1976	Waldemar Cierpinski	GDR	**2:09:55**
1980	Waldemar Cierpinski	GDR	**2:11:03**

European Champions

Date	Runner	Nation	Time
1934	Armas Toivonen	Finland	**2:52:29**
1938	Vaino Mulnonen	Finland	**2:37:28.8**
1946	Mikko Hietanen	Finland	**2:24:55**
1950	Jack Holden	Britain	**2:32:13.2**
1954	Veikko Karvonen	Finland	**2:24:51.6**
1958	Sergey Popov	Soviet Union	**2:15:17**
1962	Brian Kilby	Britain	**2:23:18.8**
1966	James Hogan	Britain	**2:20:04.6**
1969	Ron Hill	Britain	**2:16:47.8**
1971	Karel Lismont	Belgium	**2:13:09**
1974	Ian Thompson	Britain	**2:13:18.8**
1978	Leonid Moiseyev	Soviet Union	**2:11:57.5**

Pan American Games Champions

Date	Runner	Nation	Time
1951	Delfo Cabrera	Argentina	**2:35:00.2**
1955	Doroteo Flores	Guatemala	**2:59:09.2**
1959	John Kelley	USA	**2:27:54.2**
1963	Fidel Negrete	Mexico	**2:27:55.6**
1967	Andrew Boychuk	Canada	**2:23:01.4**
1971	Frank Shorter	USA	**2:22:40**
1975	Rigoberto Mendoza	Cuba	**2:25:02.9**
1979	Radames Gonzalez	Cuba	**2:24:07**

PROGRESSION OF WORLD MEN'S RECORD

On courses accepted to have been standard distance only

Date	Runner	Nation	Time	Place
24 Jul 1908	John Hayes	US	**2:55:18.4**	London
1 Jan 1909	Robert Fowler	US	**2:52:45.4**	New York
12 Feb 1909	James Clark	US	**2:46:52.6**	New York
8 May 1909	Albert Raines	US	**2:46:04.6**	New York
26 May 1913	Harry Barrett	GB	**2:42:31**	London
12 May 1913	Harry Green	GB	**2:38:16.2**	London
31 May 1913	Alexis Ahlgren	Swe	**2:36:06.6**	London
22 Aug 1920	Johannes Kolehmainen	Fin	**2:32:35.8**	Antwerp
12 Oct 1925	Albert Michelsen	US	**2:29:01.8**	Pt Ches
31 Mar 1935	Fusashige Suzuki	Jap	**2:27:49**	Tokyo
3 Apr 1935	Yasuo Ikenaka	Jap	**2:26:44**	Tokyo
3 Nov 1935	Kitei Son	Jap	**2:26:42**	Tokyo
19 Apr 1947	Yun Bok Suh	Kor	**2:25:39**	Boston
14 Jun 1952	Jim Peters	GB	**2:20:42.2**	Chiswick
13 Jun 1953	Jim Peters	GB	**2:18:40.2**	Chiswick
4 Oct 1953	Jim Peters	GB	**2:18:34.8**	Turku
26 Jun 1954	Jim Peters	GB	**2:17:39.4**	Chiswick
24 Aug 1958	Sergey Popov	SU	**2:15:17**	Stockholm
10 Sep 1960	Abebe Bikila	Eth	**2:15:16.2**	Rome
17 Feb 1963	Toru Terasawa	Jap	**2:15:15.8**	Beppu
15 Jun 1963	Leonard Edelen	US	**2:14:28**	Chiswick
13 Jun 1964	Basil Heatley	GB	**2:13:55**	Chiswick
21 Oct 1964	Abebe Bikila	Eth	**2:12:11.2**	Tokyo
12 Jun 1965	Morio Shigematus	Jap	**2:12:00**	Chiswick
3 Dec 1967	Derek Clayton	Aust	**2:09:36.4**	Fukuoka
30 May 1969	Derek Clayton	Aust	**2:08:33.6**	Antwerp
25 Oct 1981	Alberto Salazar	US	**2:08:13**	New York

PROGRESSION OF WOMEN'S WORLD RECORD

Date	Runner	Nation	Time	Place
23 May 1964	Dale Greig	GB	**3:27:45**	Ryde, Eng
21 Jul 1964	Mildred Sampson	NZ	**3:19:33**	Auckland
6 May 1967	Maureen Wilton	Can	**3:15:22**	Toronto

16 Sep 1967	Anni Pede-Erdkamp	GFR	**3:07:26**	Waldniel
28 Feb 1970	Caroline Walker	US	**3:02:53**	Seaside, US
9 May 1971	Elizabeth Bonner	US	**3:01:42**	Philadelphia
31 Aug 1971	Adrienne Beames	Aust	**2:46:30**	Werribee
27 Oct 1974	Chantal Langlace	France	**2:46:24**	Neuf Brisach
1 Dec 1974	Jacqueline Hansen	US	**2:43:54.5**	Culver City
21 Apr 1975	Liane Winter	GFR	**2:42:24**	Boston
3 May 1975	Christa Vahlensieck	GFR	**2:40:15.8**	Dulmen, Ger
12 Oct 1975	Jacqueline Hansen	US	**2:38:19**	Eugene, US
1 May 1977	Chantal Langlace	France	**2:35:15.4**	Oyarzun, Fra
10 Sep 1977	Christa Vahlensieck	GFR	**2:34:47.5**	West Berlin
22 Oct 1978	Greta Waitz	Norway	**2:32:29.8**	New York
21 Oct 1979	Greta Waitz	Norway	**2:27:32.6**	New York
26 Oct 1980	Greta Waitz	Norway	**2:25:41.3**	New York
25 Oct 1981	Allison Roe	NZ	**2:25:29**	New York

NATIONAL RECORDS, MEN

Nation	**Runner**	**Time**	**Year**
Algeria	Abedlmadjid Mada	**2:15:01**	1980
Argentina	Alfredo Maravilla	**2:17:43**	1981
Australia	Derek Clayton	**2:08:34**	1969
Austria	Josef Steiner	**2:16:43**	1980
Belgium	Marc Smet	**2:10:00**	1979
Brazil	Eloy Rodriguez-Scheider	**2:14:54**	1981
Canada	Jerome Drayton	**2:10:09**	1975
China	Xu Liang	**2:13:32**	1980
Columbia	Victor Mora-Garcia	**2:12:55**	1981
Cuba	Radames Gonzalez	**2:16:15**	1980
Czechoslovakia	Vlastimil Zwiefelhofer	**2:14:19**	1980
Denmark	Jorn Lauenborg	**2:13:45**	1980
Eire	Louis Kenny	**2:12:21**	1980
Finland	Esa Tikkanen	**2:11:15**	1978
France	Jean-Michel Charbonnet	**2:12:18**	1980
GDR	Waldemar Cierpinski	**2:09:55**	1976

GFR	Werner Dorrenbacher	**2:12:22**	1980
Great Britain	Ian Thompson	**2:09:12**	1974
Greece	Michael Koussis	**2:14:42**	1978
Hungary	Ferenc Szekeres	**2:12:35**	1980
India	Shivnath Singh	**2:12:00**	1978
Italy	Guiseppe Cindolo	**2:11:45**	1975
Japan	Shigeru Soh	**2:09:06**	1978
Kenya	Joseph Kingebi	**2:16:31**	1976
Mexico	Rofolfo Gomez	**2:10:14**	1980
Netherlands	Gerard Nijboer	**2:09:01**	1980
North Korea	Chun Son Goe	**2:10:52**	1980
New Zealand	Dick Quax	**2:10:47**	1980
Poland	Jerzy Gross	**2:13:05**	1975
Rumania	Catalin Andreica	**2:12:30**	1978
South Africa	Geoff Bacon	**2:12:10**	1980
Soviet Union	Vladimir Kotov	**2:10:58**	1980
Spain	Eleuterio Anton	**2:14:32**	1980
Sweden	Tommy Persson	**2:11:02**	1980
Switzerland	Richard Umberg	**2:14:28**	1980
Turkey	Veli Balii	**2:11:30**	1976
USA	Bill Rodgers	**2:09:27**	1979

These records were correct on September 1, 1981 but on October 25 Alberto Salazar improved the US record to 2:08:13, Jukka Toivola improved the Finnish record to 2:10:53, Ryszard Marczak improved the Polish record to 2:11:36 and S. Chebor improved the Kenyan record to 2:16:00.

NATIONAL RECORDS, WOMEN

Nation	Runner	Time	Year
Australia	Elizabeth Hassall	**2:39:48**	1979
Belgium	Magda Hands	**2:41:22**	1980
Brazil	Eleonora Mendonca	**2:48:45**	1975
Canada	Jacqueline Gareau	**2:30:58**	1980

Denmark	Dorthe Rasmussen	**2:40:36**	1980
Eire	Carey May	**2:42:11**	1980
France	Chantal Langlace	**2:35:16**	1977
GFR	Charlotte Teske	**2:33:13**	1981
Great Britain	Joyce Smith	**2:29:57**	1981
Italy	Silvana Cruciata	**2:44:31**	1980
Japan	Nanae Sasaki	**2:40:56**	1981
Netherlands	Marja Wokke	**2:32:29**	1980
New Zealand	Allison Roe	**2:26:46**	1981
Norway	Greta Waitz	**2:25:42**	1980
South Africa	Sonja Laxton	**2:43:49**	1980
Soviet Union	Lyubov Putilova	**2:39:01**	1980
Spain	Iciar Martinez	**2:47:12**	1981
Sweden	Midde Hamrin	**2:43:04**	1981
Switzerland	Vreni Forster	**2:35:57**	1980
USA	Patti Catalano	**2:27:51**	1981

These records were correct on September 1 1981 but on October 25 1981 Allison Roe improved NZ record to 2:25:29, Laura Fogli improved the Italian record to 2:34:48 and Karoline Nemetz improved the Swedish record to 2:37:06.

NATIONAL ALL-COMERS RECORDS (to October 25, 1981)

Fastest marathons run in some of the major running nations:

Nation	**Runner**	**Time**	**Place**	**Year**
UK	Ron Hill (GB)	**2:09:28**	Edinburgh	1970
US	Alberto Salazar (US)	**2:08:13**	New York	1981
Holland	Gerard Nijboer (Holl)	**2:09:01**	Amsterdam	1980
Belgium	Derek Clayton (Aust)	**2:08:33.6**	Antwerp	1969
NZ	Ian Thompson (GB)	**2:09:12**	Christchurch	1974
Canada	Waldemar Cierpinski (GDR)	**2:09:55**	Montreal	1976
USSR	Vladimir Kotov (SU)	**2:10:58**	Moscow	1980
Japan	Shigeru Soh (Japan)	**2:09:05.6**	Beppu	1978
France	Chun Son Goe (N. Korea)	**2:10:52**	Essonne	1980

WORLD RECORDS FOR ALL AGES

Age	Time	Men	Time	Woman
16	**2:23:47**	M. Kingery (USA)	**2:51:48**	M. Kaput (USA)
17	**2:23:05**	C. Devery (USA)	**2:46:46**	I. Griffiths (USA)
18	**2:17:44**	K. Pfeffer (USA)	**2:39:48**	G. Volk (USA)
19	**2:15:36**	J. Eberding (GDR)	**2:40:36**	D. Rasmussen (Den)
20	**2:31:59**	D. Sagure (USA)	**2:41:44**	B. Guerin (USA)
21	**2:12:19**	D. Faircloth (GB)	**2:35:15**	J. Benoit (USA)
22	**2:09:41**	A. Salazar (USA)	**2:30:12**	J. Shea (USA)
23	**2:08:13**	A. Salazar (USA)	**2:32:29**	M. Wokke (Holl)
24	**2:09:01**	G. Nijboer (Holl)	**2:34:25**	I. Christiansen (Nor)
25	**2:09:06**	S. Soh (Japan)	**2:25:29**	A. Roe (NZ)
26	**2:08:34**	D. Clayton (Aust)	**2:27:33**	L. Moller (NZ)
27	**2:09:49**	T. Soh (Japan)	**2:25:42**	G. Waitz (Nor)
28	**2:10:00**	M. Smet (Belg)	**2:34:48**	C. Vahlensieck (GFR)
29	**2:10:14**	R. Gomez (Mex)	**2:37:29**	J. Audibert (GFR)
30	**2:10:09**	J. Drayton (Can)	**2:36:47**	C. Vahlensieck (GFR)
31	**2:09:27**	B. Rodgers (USA)	**2:38:10**	M. Angenvoorth (GFR)
32	**2:10:47**	D. Quax (NZ)	**2:39:22**	L. Binder (USA)
33	**2:12:35**	F. Szekeres (Hung)	**2:38:10**	L. Binder (USA)
34	**2:12:17**	V. Bugrov (SU)	**2:43:02**	S. Peterson (USA)
35	**2:11:36**	R. Marczak (Pol)	**2:39:48**	E. Hassall (Aust)
36	**2:12:35**	R. Hill (GB)	**2:35:05**	C. Gould (GB)
37	**2:13:44**	A. Wood (GB)	**2:37:26**	C. Gould (GB)
38	**2:12:10**	C. Bacon (USA)	**2:45:00**	B. Shingles (NZ)
39	**2:13:43**	J. Foster (NZ)	**2:39:33**	C. Dalrymple (USA)
40	**2:14:54**	J. Foster (NZ)	**2:47:45**	M. Gorman (USA)
41	**2:11:19**	J. Foster (NZ)	**2:36:37**	J. Smith (GB)
42	**2:18:24**	J. Foster (NZ)	**2:33:32**	J. Smith (GB)
43	**2:16:07**	J. Foster (NZ)	**2:29:56**	J. Smith (GB)
44	**2:17:54**	J. Foster (NZ)	**2:54:09**	M. Gorman (USA)
45	**2:22:06**	J. Foster (NZ)	**2:57:41**	N. Hobson (USA)
46	**2:17:29**	J. Foster (NZ)	**3:00:13**	N. Hobson (USA)
47	**2:20:55**	E. Ostybe (Swe)	**3:04:55**	N. Hobson (USA)
48	**2:22:40**	P. Alphen (Holl)	**3:04:19**	R. Anderson (USA)
49	**2:23:55**	J. Foster (NZ)	**2:58:11**	T. D'Elia (USA)
50	**2:22:49**	P. Alphen (Holl)	**2:57:25**	T. D'Elia (USA)

51	**2:25:19**	E. Ostybe (Swe)	**3:18:48**	M. Miller (USA)
52	**2:31:30**	E. Ostybe (Swe)	**3:14:20**	M. Miller (USA)
53	**2:29:20**	E. Ostybe (Swe)	**3:05:02**	M. Miller (USA)
54	**2:34:43**	E. Ostybe (Swe)	**3:03:28**	M. Miller (USA)
55	**2:26:35**	E. Ostybe (Swe)	**3:18:07**	H. Dick (USA)
56	**2:27:05**	E. Ostybe (Swe)	**3:09:47**	H. Dick (USA)
57	**2:42:00**	E. Ostybe (Swe)	**3:27:55**	M. Trent (USA)
58	**2:50:14**	J. Gilmore (Aust)	**3:51:18**	E. Tuinzing (USA)
59	**2:38:19**	J. Gilmore (Aust)	**3:32:28**	L. Schultz (GFR)
60	**2:47:46**	C. Davies (USA)	**3:21:35**	L. Schultz (GFR)

Fastest known by runners over 70 are: men — W. Hayward (S.Africa) 3:06:24; women — M. Lindgren (US) 4:37:37. Fastest over 80, men — P. Spangler (US) 4:23:55.

BRITISH MARATHONS 1982

(excluding those recorded in Chapter 6, 'Running Around the World'.)

MARCH

14

Winchester: P. Brentnall, 17 Romsey Rd, Winchester, Hants.
British-American: E. Barrett, 129 Thisselt Rd, Canvey Island, Essex (Canvey Is 618643 day).

28

Guildford: D. Sadler, 7 Boxgrove Lane, Guildford, Surrey.
Wolverhampton: B. Wilson, 60 Tettenhall Road, Wolverhampton (0902-20885).
Horsforth Metro: Mrs J. Kitchen, 15 West End Close, Horsforth, Leeds (0532-587294 evenings).

APRIL

4

Gosport and Fareham: H. Pritchard, 42 High St., Gosport, Hants (07017-84271).

Mid-Wales: D. Rice, Snowdonia School of Adventure, Barmouth, Gwynedd.
Stockport Daffodil: Recreation Division, Town Hall, Stockport, Cheshire. (061-480-4949).

11

Southampton: Mayor's Secretary. Mayor's Parlour. Civic Centre, Southampton. (0703-23855).
Huddersfield Chippindale: J. Sawyer, Shieling, 1 Pennine View, Kirkheaton, Huddersfield, W. Yorks.

18

Basingstoke: J. Blake, 78 Copland Close, Brighton Hill, Basingstoke, Hants (0256-61131).
Isle of Thanet: T. Cella, Recreation Dept, Hartsdown House, Hantsdown Park, Margate, Kent (0843-25511 day).

28

RAF Swinderby (service and ex-service personnel only): Fl-Lt Sanderson, OC PED Flight, RAF Swinderby, Lincoln.

MAY

3

Abingdon: M. Cooper, Wick Hall, Radley, Abingdon, Oxon.
Norfolk: H. Dick-Cleland, Anglia Building Society, 20 Castle Meadow, Norwich (0603-613605 day).

23

Kingsword Festival: P. Forward, Leisure Services, Kingswood District Council, Warmley House, Tower Rd North, Kingswood, Bristol (0272-61161 ext 286 day).

29

Foyle Festival: G. Lynch, Templemore Sports Complex, Buncrana Rd, Londonderry, NI (0504-65521 day).

JUNE

6

Sheffield: Richard Hnat Sports, 148 Infirmary Rd, Sheffield (0742-731413).

13

AAA Championships, Gateshead: AAA, Francis House, Francis St., London SW1 (men only).

20

Three Forts, Sussex: D. Bradstreet, 60 Graham Ave, Portslade, Sussex (not a road course).

Around the Towns, Staffs: Kevin Donovan, The Place, Hanley, Stoke on Trent (0782-25071).

JULY

11

Southend Access: Ted Lewin, 19 Little Thorpe, Thorpe Bay, Southend, Essex (0702-586359 evenings).

North Tyneside: G. Chester, Town Hall, High St East, Wallsend, Tyne & Wear (0632-627371 day).

AUGUST

8

Newcastle-upon-Tyne: Newcastle Evening Chronicle, Thomson House, Groat Market, Newcastle (0632-27500).

29

Inverclyde Folk: D. Hodelet, Inverclyde District Council, Municipal Buildings, Greenock (0475-34762).

Nuneaton Hospitals: A. Gammie, Path Lab, George Eliot Hospital, Nuneaton, Warks (0203-384201 ext 467 day).

SEPTEMBER

5

Wear Valley: Lewis McEldon, Wear Valley District Council, Crook, Co Durham (0388-763121 day).

19

Rotherham: D. Haywood, 14 Whitehill Rd, Brinsworth, Rotherham S. Yorks (0709-70668).

Birmingham Interplas: T. Colton, Sports Cellar, 212 Pool Road, Leicester. (0533-59504)

26

Leicester Charities: I. Davidson, Castles Garage, Dover St, Leicester (0533-556262).

Cardiff: Bernie Plain, 6 Four Elms Rd, Roath, Cardiff (0222-492520).

OCTOBER

3

Robin Hood, Nottingham: H. Taylor, Leisure Services, Notts County Council, Trent Bridge House, Fox Rd, West Bridgford, Nottingham (0602-866555 ext 325).

North Wales: Pat Evans, 17 Fford Pendyffryn, Prestatyn, Clwyd.

9

Cumbria Lakes: D. Wells, Cockermouth Sports Centre, Castlegate Drive, Cockermouth, Cumbria (0900-823596).

10

Masters' and Maidens', Guildford: R. Smith, 14 Amberwood Rise, New Malden, Surrey (01-949 2720).

Huntingdon: M. Paulson, Peterborough Building Society, High St, Huntingdon, Cambs (0480-57156 day).

17

Honiton: M. Stone, 24 Jerrard Crescent, Honiton, Devon (0404-41382).

23

Black Isle: D. Watt, Rosshire Journal, Castle St, Dingwall, Scotland (0349-63436 day).

24

Harlow: T. Dradey, The Maples, Harlow, Essex (04023-46681).

Chesterfield: S. Brailey, North Derbyshire Squash Club, Old Road, Chesterfield, Derby (0246-77760).

31

Leeds: N. Littlewood, Fearnville Sports Centre, Oakwood Lane, Leeds 8 (0532-720121).

This list courtesy of *Running* magazine.